Designing
for the
KNITTING
MACHINE

Bea Poulter

Designing
for the
KNITTING
MACHINE

Bea Poulter

B T Batsford Limited, London

To my parents, Mary and Harold Suttle,
who taught me the joy of learning

ISBN 0 7134 5533 0

Typeset by
Latimer Trend & Company Ltd, Plymouth
and printed in Great Britain by
Anchor Brendon Ltd
Tiptree, Essex

for the publishers
B. T. Batsford Ltd
4 Fitzhardinge Street
London W1H 0AH

The photography is by Vernon Poulter

Contents

ACKNOWLEDGEMENT

I would like to thank the following:

Jones Sewing Machine Co. Limited, for giving me the opportunity to use their Brother KH 910 electronic machine.

Knitmaster Limited, for the use of their 700 punchcard machine.

Nantiago Yarns, Silverknit Yarns, Atkinsons Yarns, Jamieson and Smith and Simply Shetland, for letting me have a selection of their lovely yarns for use on the designs.

My grateful thanks to my husband, Vernon, for his patience over the photographs, and to my daughter Susan Calverley for typing the manuscript.

Also thank you to Hilary, Susan, Ria, Shaun, Andrew, Mark, Peter and Thomas for modelling the garments.

ABBREVIATIONS USED IN THE PATTERNS

COR	carriage on right
COL	carriage on left
beg	beginning
approx	approximately
MT	main tension
MT−1	main tension minus one whole number (tighter)
MT+1	main tension plus one whole number (looser)
WP	working position
NWP	non-working position
UWP	upper working position
HP	holding position
RC	row counter
WY	waste yarn
cm	centimetre
in.	inch
gm	gram
alt	alternate
inc	increase
dec	decrease
st(s)	stitch(es)
st st	stocking stitch
carr	carriage

INTRODUCTION

Like many people I was first attracted to machine knitting by the speed and economy with which I could clothe my family. Once hooked, I realized that speed is not everything and that it is a very creative craft. I will never knit all the possible combinations of patterns, so I am always learning.

The aim of this book is to encourage you to have the confidence to experiment for yourself. I have shown some ways of varying the patterns and I hope they will spark off new ideas of your own. You should be able to translate your ideas into machine knitting techniques which will give you the result you want.

All the designs in this book can be knitted on the single bed, standard gauge machine. If you have a ribbing attachment then you can substitute true ribs for the welts or hems where applicable, or they can be knitted onto the garment afterwards by hand. Knitting them first and transferring to the machine puts strain on the stitches; they will not always stretch across the machine needles, so knit the last row on a larger size of knitting needle.

The instructions in chapter 2 for making the block pattern are quite detailed because all the other shapes and styles can be adapted from it. If you understand how to make a garment fit properly, then you will understand how to alter it to your design.

The punchcards are designed for a 24-stitch repeat. They can be drawn onto the sheet for the electronic machines, only one complete repeat of the pattern being necessary for this. Take care that the last row of the pattern is not also the first row of the next. Many patterns can be knitted by manual selection or by earlier punchbutton models.

I have included instructions for hand finishing in the patterns. When I am sitting at the machine I like to *knit* as much as I can – for example I avoid casting off long lengths on the machine as it takes time (and is not very interesting), I prefer to take the knitting off onto the waste yarn and then I can sit in the garden or in front of the television to graft shoulders, or turn down neckbands. You may prefer to pick up stitches and cast off on the machine – we all have our favourite methods.

What is obvious to one may be obscure to another, so there is a mixture of simple and more difficult designs. This book is not intended to replace your instruction manual – the basic methods of using your particular model should be learnt from the manual.

The notes for each pattern include instructions which apply to all garments. I have described ways of following them that I found to be the easiest and which will give good results.

The versatility of the knitting machine is amazing. You are in control – now make the machine do whatever *you* want.

CHAPTER I

Tools of the trade

Knitting machines

All modern machines are capable of knitting similar patterns but they have different knobs and levers to produce them. Knitmaster machines are a little different from others as their carriage will select patterning needles and knit them on the same row. Brother, Toyota and Singer preselect the needles and push the needles forward to upper working position on the row before those particular needles will be knitted so that you can see which needles will knit in pattern on the next row. This means that sometimes the techniques are slightly different for each machine, although the end result is the same.

It is important to keep your machine clean. Oily, sticky lumps of fluff will not help it to perform at its best. Always brush all the fluff away from the needle bed after working each piece of knitting. This will help to stop the build-up of fluff inside the machine and around the needle bed and will not spoil the next garment. If you knit a jumper in dark green wool and the next piece is a pale pink dress, the minute specks of dark wool will soon attach themselves to the new knitting and produce dirty marks that will not wash out.

Do not be too liberal with the oil. The needle butts need a very thin film of oil to ease their way through the complicated pattern of cams under the carriage, but a drop of oil on a cloth wiped over them is enough. About twice a year take all the needles out of the bed, vacuum the bed and pick all the fluff out with an old needle. Do this gently. Do not poke down too much inside or you may damage springs underneath. Wash the needles in surgical spirit, rubbing them to get the oil off, and leave them on paper towels to dry thoroughly. Do not wash off the spirit. The needles will be left with a trace of oil on them which helps them to knit. The machine will knit like new when they are replaced. This procedure is well worth the trouble.

Some of the faults that can occur

1 *All the stitches dropping off* This will only happen if there is no yarn being taken across the needles. Either it has broken, or it is incorrectly threaded into the carriage. Ensure that it is in the right feeder and, if the machine has one, that the gate to keep it in place is closed.

2 *Stitches building up on a needle* This is caused by a faulty needle – either the latch or the hook is bent. The needles are easily replaced. There is a needle-retaining bar which is withdrawn, the needle is removed backwards with latch closed and the new one is inserted from the back with the latch open so that it does not catch in the bed (see your instruction manual for details). This change can be made even when there is knitting on the machine – transfer the stitch temporarily to the next needle.

3 *Loops at the ends of the rows* Make sure the yarn mast is correctly threaded or it will not hold the yarn under sufficient tension at the end of the row.

Loops can also be caused by knitting too quickly, taking the carriage well beyond the end of the needle bed and bringing it back so fast that the tension mast does not have time to take up the tension. The yarn loops onto the brushes underneath the carriage and does not knit into the first needle.

Sometimes one of the sinker pins, between the needles, is slightly bent and the yarn catches on this. It can be carefully eased back into line with pliers.

4 *Dropped stitches at the edges* These can be caused by an incorrectly threaded tension mast. If the tension is too tight, the end needles will pull forward at the ends of the rows and the stitches do not knit on the next row.

A too tight carriage tension for the yarn being used may make the edge stitches very tight and they drop off.

If the edge stitches are not pulling over the needles properly more weight is needed on the edge stitches – hang a claw weight at the edge, and move it up every 5–10cm (2–4 in.)

If a bent needle is not knitting the stitch, replace it.

5 *Dropped stitches in the centre* These are usually caused by a faulty needle. Replace the needle and continue to knit. If the stitch has dropped down many rows it is easier to pick it up with the latch tool after the work is finished and graft-stitch it into position. If it has only dropped a couple of rows, put the transfer tool into the row beneath it, and place stitch and all the loops from the lost rows onto the needle. Knit them through one by one.

6 *Loops catching on the sinker pins* These result in the knitting bunching up and pushing stitches off the needles. This seems to happen even when the sinker pins are perfectly in line. If it is possible without spoiling the pattern, push the needles nearest to the bunching to holding position – this stops the stitches from coming off the needles. Hook the latch tool into the threads on the sinkers and pull them up and off the top. The work will then drop down. Sometimes this happens when the tension is very loose, when a thread floats over the sinker, or when using a tuck-stitch pattern with many loops on one needle.

If you undo a row of knitting, look carefully to see that none of the stitches has looped onto the sinkers as you pull the yarn out of the needle.

Yarns

The yarns used for each pattern in this book are described and are all easily available at the time of publication from shops or by mail order (see list of suppliers at the end of the book). However, you may have your own ideas on varying the look of a garment and suggestions are made for other yarns which will knit to the same tension, where possible. You should try out your own yarns by sampling them. If you can knit to the tension stated in the pattern and get a fabric with the right 'feel' to it, then it will be quite suitable.

Coned yarns are ideal for machine knitting as they are all waxed and ready to use at the smooth speed needed for the machine. There is a huge variety available and many suppliers give the thickness in the equivalent 'ply' with which most people are familiar from hand knitting, but if you use industrial yarns, perhaps from a market, which have been produced for the knitwear factories, then the thickness is measured by the 'count'. This count is the length of yarn of that thickness which will weigh a given amount. There are several standards in use, but in them all the higher the number of the count the thinner the yarn will be, since more of it is required to achieve the weight. Usually there are two numbers given. For example 2/36: the first number, 2, indicates the number of strands that are twisted together, and the second number, 36, is the count number.

The following list will give you some idea of the different counts equivalent to a ply.

2/30 is a fine 2-ply yarn equivalent to a 1½-ply handknitting measure
Two strands of 2/30 = 3-ply
Three strands   = 4-ply
Four strands   = double knitting

2/14 is a fine 2-ply
Two strands of 2/14 = 4 ply

2/16 is a full 2-ply yarn (lambswool is usually 2/16)

Two strands of 2/26 = a full 4-ply

2/8 is a 4-ply yarn equivalent (Shetland wool is 2/8)

These many fine yarns can be doubled, trebled or multiplied further to give not only different thicknesses but also new colours and textures. Two or three strands of 2/30 in different colours knitted together will give a tweed effect, and with a textured stitch such as tuck pattern it is particularly interesting. When mixing colours in this way, in order to avoid stripes of one colour dominating, the threads can be run through the centres of the other cones by standing the cones one above another on boxes (a 'cake stand'). The threads then wind round one another more evenly. As the bottom strand comes through the centre of the cone, the second strand unwinds to twist round it. If these two are threaded through a

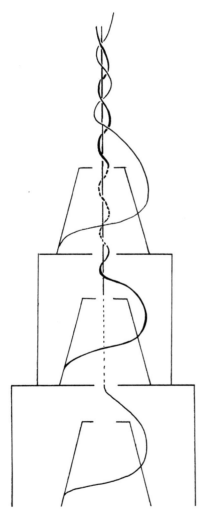

1 The 'cake stand', showing each yarn threaded through the one above, resulting in a more evenly twisted yarn. Each cone is supported on a box with a hole cut in the top

third cone then this thread will wind round the first two. Thread the yarns through the same tension wire on the yarn mast and into the same feeder on the sinker plate. In this way an even mix of colours is made before making the stitch.

Hand-knitting yarns may be used quite successfully, but they are considerably more expensive, usually have a higher twist and require more preparation before use. The balls are not designed to be used at the speed of machine knitting, and although sometimes one can pull the yarn from the centre of the ball so that it does not bounce about, it often results in knots and snarls. *Never* take the yarn from the outside of a commercially wound ball of yarn as it will jerk about as you knit, giving very uneven stitches, perhaps breaking, and tangling round your feet. The yarn really needs to be rewound on a wool winder to give a cake which stands flat on the table or floor, and the yarn can be drawn smoothly from the centre. When the yarn is removed from the spindle of the winder, as it relaxes the centre of the ball sometimes closes up very tightly, so the yarn has to be pulled quite hard from the centre. To prevent this happening, thread the balls onto a piece of dowel, or even a pencil, so that as the yarn relaxes the centre of the ball is kept open.

Before knitting, knot the end of each ball to the beginning of the next. It is better to have to unravel part of a row to get rid of a knot than to have all the knitting fall onto your feet because you did not realize you were near the end of the ball. It also means that you will not have to stop to rethread every ball through the yarn mast.

Textured yarns such as a bouclé will knit up thicker than a smoother yarn of a similar ply/count, because the nature of the yarn prevents it from making an even stitch. More rows will be needed and probably fewer stitches, as the stitches are pushed apart by the uneven yarn.

Mohair and other brushed yarns sometimes cause problems by getting caught up by their hairs on the sinker pins. This can be made less of a problem by putting the yarn in a refrigerator (or even the freezer!) overnight – the hairs do not fluff out so much when they are cold. Every few rows it is necessary to give a sharp tug down on the knitting to break the hairs which are caught on the sinker pins. Otherwise you will find the knitting will eventually bunch up so much that stitches will start to be pushed off the needles and will not knit properly. It makes a rather frightening tearing noise as you pull the work down but does not seem to harm the finished fabric, or the machine.

Shetland wool is spun in oil which gives it a rather stringy appearance. It needs to be knitted at a looser tension than that used normally for wool of that thickness. After washing it will fluff out.

Tension swatches

Most hand knitters never make a tension swatch before beginning a garment, but because they can measure the work as they go along and judge almost as soon as they start whether it is about right for size then it doesn't matter too much. On a knitting machine, though, it does matter. Because the work is stretched out across the needles it is quite impossible to measure the knitting while it is on the machine. So it is vital for the success of a garment that you knit a swatch first, not only to measure the number of stitches and rows but also to assess whether the texture and feel of the knitting, and the stitch pattern, are suitable for the garment you want to make. Fortunately, unlike hand knitting, the tension swatch can be done quickly, although the result cannot be measured immediately.

Because of the stretching effect of the machine, the swatch must be allowed to rest for a while in order for the yarn to relax into its normal state. Give the knitting a good pull lengthways to pull the stitches closer together and leave it for at least an hour, longer if possible. If you wish to knit in the evening, try to find ten minutes in the morning to knit one or more swatches which can be measured later. The swatch must be treated exactly as you will treat the finished garment. It should be pressed, with or without steam, according to the type of yarn and the type of finish you want. If you are using oiled Shetland wool then the swatch must be washed and pressed, because you will need to wash any garment knitted in Shetland wool before it is worn.

The larger the piece of knitting that can be measured, the more accurate the tension arrived at will be. Do not cast on fewer than 50 stitches and knit at least 60 rows. Measure the stitches and rows in the centre of the swatch (stitches near the edge may be slightly distorted). The tension can be measured over 5cm, 10cm (2 in., 4 in.), etc., but a more accurate result will be achieved by measuring a set number of stitches.

Charters

The swatch required by charting devices is 40 stitches wide and 60 rows long, so even if you do not own a charter now this is a good size to work to. The Knitmaster Green Ruler used over these numbers will give you an accurate number of stitches/rows per 10cm (4 in.). These rulers are supplied with the Knitrader, but can be bought separately from many knitting machine suppliers. Instructions are given with the ruler, but remember that the numbers shown on it are not a measurement in themselves – they only tell you the number of stitches and rows in every 10cm (4 in.) of knitting. For Toyota and Brother charters the readings are made with straightforward measurements in centimetres and millimetres.

Using a charting device simplifies pattern making. There are two types – one on which the pattern is drawn as it will be knitted, at full scale (Brother, Toyota), and the other which is drawn at half scale (Knitmaster). They are both used in the same way. The design is drawn onto the chart which is rolled into the machine.

To assess the number of stitches needed for a given width, one of the set of rulers is selected which corresponds to the number of stitches (or the measurement) across the swatch and placed in front of the chart. This indicates how many stitches are to be cast on. The gears of the charter are set to the number of rows (or the measurement) of the length of the swatch and will move the chart exactly the right number of rows for a given length. The chart is turned on by the row tripper and as it revolves you can see exactly where, and by how many stitches, increases and decreases are to be made.

The great advantage of this is that the same size of garment can now be knitted in any yarn, and in any stitch pattern, simply by measuring a tension swatch.

If you vary the stitch pattern for the garment, do not use a stocking stitch *written* pattern and knit it in Fair Isle or tuck stitch at the *original tension* and *number of stitches* – it will not fit. Altering the stitch pattern will make quite a big difference to the tension. Tuck stitch or weaving will push the stitches apart, so fewer stitches will be needed. Fair Isle and slip patterns have floats stretching across between knitted stitches which will pull the knitting in, and so require more stitches, at the same tension, to make the width. Fair Isle bands in a stocking-stitch garment should be knitted at a looser tension so that the knitting is not pulled in, but remember this will also reduce the number of rows needed, since the stitches are bigger. All this shows how very important the tension square is – there is no escaping it!

To knit a tension square

Choose the yarn to be used and the stitch pattern for the garment. Decide on the approximate tension to knit with the yarn chosen, either from previous experience or using an indication on the pattern to be used. If you have no idea which to use, then a series of tension squares should be knitted until you decide which tension gives you the result you want.

Cast on 60 st with WY in a good contrast colour, 30 st each side of 0. Knit a few rows. Break off yarn and rethread with MY. Set RC to 000, set tension dial to approximate tension required (e.g. 2/16, 2-ply, tension 2–4; 2/8, 4-ply, tension 6–8;

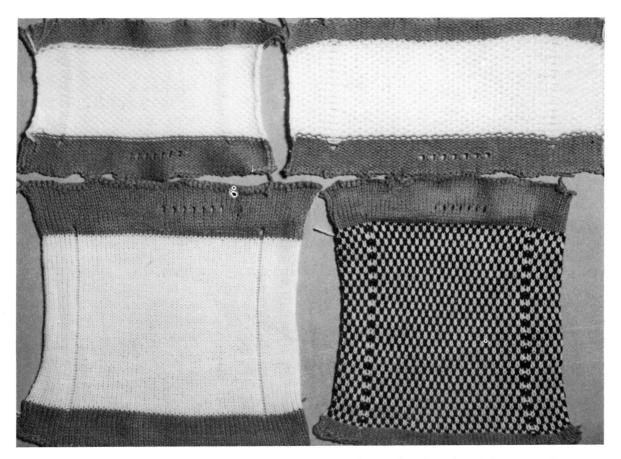

2 Tension swatches knitted from the same yarn at the same tension to show how the stitch pattern affects the size. One needle in non-working position each side of centre 40 stitches, 60 rows long. Tension marked by the holes in the waste yarn

Top left Slip stitch *Top right* Tuck stitch *Bottom left* Stocking stitch *Bottom right* Fair Isle

double knitting yarn, approximate tensions 9–10). Different tensions may be needed depending on the stitch pattern chosen. Transfer 21st st on each side of o to next needle. Leave this needle out of work throughout the square, so that a ladder forms on each side of 40 sts in the centre.
Knit 60 rows.
Change to contrast yarn, and knit about 6 rows.
Transfer alt sts to next needles – the same number as the tension dial number for MY of swatch (so at tension 7 transfer 7 alt sts; at tension 7.2, after 7th transfer leave gap of 3 needles, then transfer 2 more alt stitches). You will have a permanent record of the tension of that square (bits of paper pinned on are liable to be lost, and you will not remember the tension used).
Finish square by knitting a few more rows in WY. Remove from the machine. There is no need to cast off, but cut yarn close to last stitch – a long trailing end might get caught on something and could unravel several rows.
Wash and press swatch as necessary when it has been allowed to relax for a while.

If you want to use the designs in this book exactly as they are written, your tension must match that for the pattern. You must make your own tension square from the yarn you will use – the tension dial number given, as in all patterns, can only be used as a guide. If you are using a 4-ply acrylic similar to the one used for the design, then the tension should match up, but you may find you have to move the dial one notch either way to achieve the right tension, or even a whole number. When you have the correct tension, make sure the fabric feels right for the garment you are making. If all this matches then you can go ahead and knit the pattern as it is written, but if the yarn you are using feels too stiff or too flimsy at the tension given – and you still want to knit the garment in this yarn – you must experiment with the tension to find a fabric which is acceptable and then measure it. If the tension is very close to that given then it will not be too crucial to the size of the garment if you knit the pattern at the size given. However, if it is several stitches out then you must work out for yourself the number of stitches and rows needed to give the required size from the diagrammatic block which is given for each design.

Examples
Pattern gives 28 sts to 10cm (4 in.). Cast on 129 sts to measure 46cm (18 in.).
Your swatch gives 34 sts to 10cm (4 in.), so cast on 156 sts to measure 46cm (18 in.).

Pattern gives 40 rows for a length of 10cm (4 in.). Knit 152 rows to measure 38cm (15 in.).
Your swatch gives 48 rows for a length of 10cm (4 in.). Knit 182 rows to measure 38cm (15 in.).

CHAPTER 2

Making a basic pattern to fit

There is no such person as one with 'average' measurements. Everyone is different and you should look at the measurements given on each pattern to ensure that they are not wildly different from your own. You may need the sleeves longer, or the waist-to-armhole length shorter. Once you start to alter anything you are beginning to design your own knitwear.

Making a basic block to fit

If possible ask someone else to measure you. It is easier than trying to take your own.

Body measurements required

1 *Chest or bust* Add 5cm (2 in.) for an average-fitting garment, more of course for a 'baggy' look.

2 *Total length* (from nape of the neck to the required hip length) It is also useful to measure the length to the waist. This is needed if you make a dress.

3 *Back neck width* This always seems surprisingly small. Measure the width close in to the neck. For an adult it should be between 14cm and 16cm ($5\frac{1}{2}$ in. and $6\frac{1}{4}$ in.). If it is any wider the neck will gape at the side, and if it is any less it will not pull over the head. Although not absolutely essential the neckband will fit better if the back neck is lowered about 2cm ($\frac{3}{4}$ in.) and the sides curved up to the shoulders. This is more comfortable for an older person who may be slightly round-shouldered. For children's garments this is not necessary – the back neck can be straight across. In fact many adult garments are knitted like this for speed.

4 *Drop of the front neck* This is a matter of personal choice, but for an adult's crew-neck sweater it should not be less than 7cm ($2\frac{3}{4}$ in.) lower than the back neck. For children's garments it should be 5 or 6cm lower (2 in. approx). Any less than this for a round neck and it will not sit properly round the neck, there will be wrinkles at the shoulders and it will feel uncomfortable. The neck comes from the front of the body not the top, so even for a slashed neck, which looks straight across and is wider at the sides, it will be more comfortable to wear if the front is about 2cm ($\frac{3}{4}$ in.) lower than the back.

5 *Armhole depth* This is half the measurement taken from the shoulder edge round under the arm and back up to the shoulder. This measurement should be taken close under the arm but not too tight. For an adult the minimum depth should be not less than 18–20cm (7–8 in.).

6 *Across-chest width* (taken from shoulder to shoulder above the bust) This will be about 10cm (4 in.) less than half the chest measurement, before adding ease. Do not go over the edge of the shoulderbone with this measurement since the weight of the sleeves tends to pull the shoulders down. If the sleeves are long to start with, the garment will look as if it is hanging off the shoulders and badly fitting.

7 *Slope of the shoulders* The average drop from the neck to the shoulder edge is about 3cm (1 in.). This is not really measurable, so is taken as a standard measurement. For children about 2cm ($\frac{3}{4}$ in.) is usual.

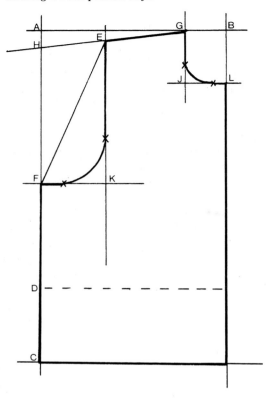

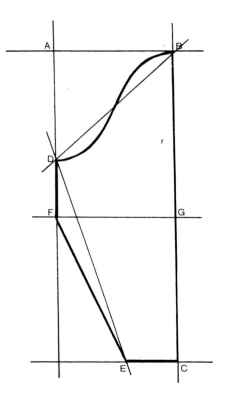

To draw the block

Construction lines are drawn first using the measurements taken. Since the garment is symmetrical it is only necessary to draw half the width of the front/back. Draw a rectangle the width of one-quarter of chest measurement plus one-quarter of ease allowed, and the length of the garment.

Slope of the shoulders is taken right to the edge of the block, lowering it 3cm (1 in.) on the edge of the across-chest width meet.

Square armhole off downwards from E and across from F.

Curve armhole by marking one-third of length from F to K (X) and one-third up from K to E (X). Draw in the curve to join these points.

Similarly draw in the curve of the neckline from a point one-third of the way along the line L to J (X) and one-third up on the line J to G (X).

Draw in the garment line firmly. The construction lines can then be rubbed out.

On this full-scale block it is possible to work out your own pattern using the tension swatch in the stitch of your choice. For example, if there are 40 stitches to 12cm ($4\frac{3}{4}$ in.), and half chest width is 46cm (18 in.), 153 stitches are needed.

The rate of the curve of the neck and of the armhole can be worked out from the tension square, using the measurement and shapes of the block. Perhaps it is worth investing in a calculator – although it is really only a matter of simple arithmetic.

3 The basic block, showing the construction lines

Body	AB = $\frac{1}{4}$ chest + $\frac{1}{4}$ total ease allowed
	AC = total length
	GB = $\frac{1}{2}$ back neck width
	BL = front neck drop
	EF = armhole depth
	EB = $\frac{1}{2}$ across-chest width
	X = $\frac{1}{3}$ measurement along line for drawing in the curve
	D = waistline
Sleeve	BC = total length
	DE = underarm length
AB and FG = $\frac{1}{2}$ width upper arm + $\frac{1}{2}$ ease
	EC = $\frac{1}{2}$ wrist
	AD = $\frac{2}{3}$ armhole depth on body

Sleeve block

Sleeve measurements required:

1 Length from shoulder to wrist, with the arm straight.

2 Length from underarm to wrist. As this will be a sloping line when knitted, add 3cm (1 in.) to this measurement.

3 Width of upper arm, above the elbow, plus 2cm (¾ in.) ease.

4 Width round the hand, over the widest part with the thumb. The cuff has to pull over the hand, so if you measure the wrist it may be too small to get on, especially if knitting in a yarn without much 'give', such as a cotton.

5 The length of the sleeve head for a set-in sleeve is about two-thirds of the length of the armhole on the body. When making the block this measurement will be made automatically from the two length measurements.

6 From above the elbow to the underarm is the widest part of the arm, so the sleeve shaping must finish about 10cm (4 in.) below the armhole shaping, so that the upper part of the sleeve is wide enough. If the sleeve is tight and the armhole not big enough, the bottom of the jumper will pull up every time the wearer moves an arm.

As with the body block, only half the width need be drawn.

To shape the sleeve head, cast off stitches equal to 1.5cm (¾ in.) to fit into the armhole shape. These few stitches will help to make the sleeve tuck in under the armpit.

Draw the rest of the sleeve head in the curve as shown in fig. 3, crossing the diagonal construction line halfway up. Some stitches will be cast off straight at the top.

Your first knitted piece can be laid on the full-size block to check the shape and verify the calculations before continuing the knitting.

This diagram can be drawn onto the sheet of a charter. Knitmaster radar owners will have to reduce all the measurements to half scale – a triangular half scale rule will make this calculation easier.

Making a hem at the bottom of a garment

If you have a ribber you may substitute true ribs for the welts and neckbands, but do read the information on making hems too, because not every garment requires a ribbed edge, and you may find the information useful another time.

Whether they are in stocking stitch or in a mock rib, hem~~~~~~~~~~~~~~~~~~~~~~~~~~~ can be ~~~~~~~~~~~~~~~~~~~~~~~~ bottom. ~~~~~~~~~~~~~~~~~~~~ line whe~~~~~~~~~~~~~~

Two ~~~~~~~~ firstly th~~~~~~~~ same ter~~~~~~~~ ing again~~~~~~~ a tight r~~~~~~~ There a~~~~~~~

1 Alway~~~~~~~ tighter te~~~~~~~ possibly ~~~~~~~

2 Knittir~~~~~~~ main yar~~~~~~~ less bulky, and so it will lie flat.

3 At the fold of the hem, knit one row much looser than the main tension. This causes the knitting to fold towards the purl side, and makes a crisp edge. (If the purl side is to be the right side of the garment, then a tight row will need to be knitted on the fold line, so that the knitting will fold towards the knit side.)

4 Probably the best way to avoid a line at the hem if you wish to pick up and finish it on the machine is to knit the first two rows of the (under) hem with sewing cotton (fig. 4). When these stitches are picked up onto the needles, the bulk is negligible, so there is no tight row.

5 If you are using the same thickness of yarn throughout, pick up the stitches from the beginning to replace them on the needles, and knit one row at about three tension points looser. This loose row gives room for the two stitches to be knitted together without pulling tight.

6 The hem stitches can be left until finishing the garment then turned up and caught down by hand.

7 *Picot hem* This is a dainty edging which

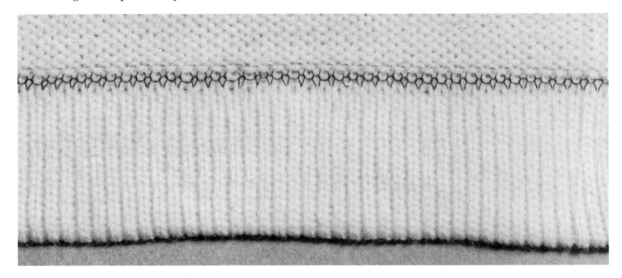

4 Hem begun with two rows of sewing cotton, shown here in a contrast colour for clarity. This helps to avoid a tight line at the hem

always looks good on baby clothes. The first half of the hem is knitted, then alternate stitches (or every third or fourth stitch) are transferred to the next needles. Leave the needles in working position and knit the loose row for the fold. Complete the hem and when it is folded in half the row of holes along the edge will make the picot edge.

8 *Mock rib hems* These should not be made by using only alternate needles, as this makes a flimsy hem. A firmer 'rib' will be made by leaving every third or fourth needle out of work.

When the hem is finished, always place a stitch onto the empty needle to avoid making a hole, by a stitch from first row of hem.

When the first rows of a mock rib are knitted with sewing cotton or a fine yarn, the stitches cannot be replaced to make the hem onto the empty needles because the stitches do not match those in the main yarn. The empty needle must be filled by lifting the stitch from the row below the adjacent needle onto the hook. Insert the transfer tool into the loop, taking care not to push the stitch above off the needles. You will find it easier to lift the bar between the stitches and place both threads onto the needle. This will show as a very small stitch on the right side, but is not unsightly.

Pattern for a basic stocking stitch jumper knitted in 4-ply (2/8)

To fit	71	76	81	86	91	96	101	107	cm
	28	30	32	34	36	38	40	42	in.
Length	44	50	56	56	58	61	61	63	cm
	17	20	22	22	23	24	24	25	in.
Sleeve length	35	42	43	43	45	46	46	46	cm
	14	16	17	17	17½	18	18	18	in.

Materials 300–380 gm 4-ply acrylic

Tension 28 sts and 40 rows to 10cm (4 in.) at MT approx 8

PATTERN NOTES

1 Figure 6 shows the basic shape knitted in three colours. The colours are changed at one-third and two-thirds of the total number of rows knitted.

2 When knitting with the sewing cotton after the nylon cord, hold the knitting down with one hand as you knit. The cotton and the cord are springy and the stitches could jump off the needles.

3 Knot the ends of the cotton together at the end of the row.

4 By keeping the back neck stitches in holding position, or by casting them off before the rows which are knitted to shape the shoulders, the back neck will be set below the level of the shoulders.

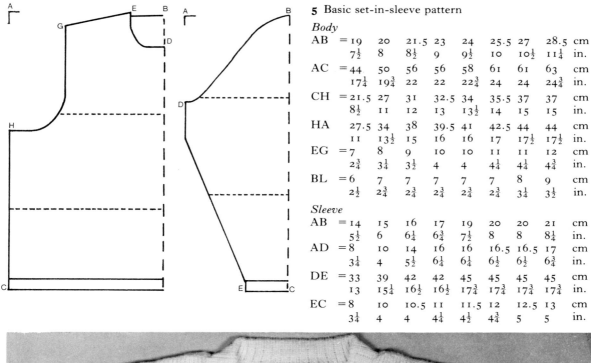

5 Basic set-in-sleeve pattern

Body

AB	=	19	20	21.5	23	24	25.5	27	28.5	cm
		$7\frac{1}{2}$	8	$8\frac{1}{2}$	9	$9\frac{1}{2}$	10	$10\frac{1}{2}$	$11\frac{1}{4}$	in.
AC	=	44	50	56	56	58	61	61	63	cm
		$17\frac{1}{4}$	$19\frac{3}{4}$	22	22	$22\frac{3}{4}$	24	24	$24\frac{3}{4}$	in.
CH	=	21.5	27	31	32.5	34	35.5	37	37	cm
		$8\frac{1}{2}$	11	12	13	$13\frac{1}{2}$	14	15	15	in.
HA	=	27.5	34	38	39.5	41	42.5	44	44	cm
		11	$13\frac{1}{2}$	15	16	16	17	$17\frac{1}{2}$	$17\frac{1}{2}$	in.
EG	=	7	8	9	10	10	11	11	12	cm
		$2\frac{3}{4}$	$3\frac{1}{4}$	$3\frac{1}{2}$	4	4	$4\frac{1}{4}$	$4\frac{1}{4}$	$4\frac{3}{4}$	in.
BL	=	6	7	7	7	7	7	8	9	cm
		$2\frac{1}{2}$	$2\frac{3}{4}$	$2\frac{3}{4}$	$2\frac{3}{4}$	$2\frac{3}{4}$	$2\frac{3}{4}$	$3\frac{1}{4}$	$3\frac{1}{2}$	in.

Sleeve

AB	=	14	15	16	17	19	20	20	21	cm
		$5\frac{1}{2}$	6	$6\frac{1}{4}$	$6\frac{3}{4}$	$7\frac{1}{2}$	8	8	$8\frac{1}{4}$	in.
AD	=	8	10	14	16	16	16.5	16.5	17	cm
		$3\frac{1}{4}$	4	$5\frac{1}{2}$	$6\frac{1}{4}$	$6\frac{1}{4}$	$6\frac{1}{2}$	$6\frac{1}{2}$	$6\frac{3}{4}$	in.
DE	=	33	39	42	42	45	45	45	45	cm
		13	$15\frac{1}{4}$	$16\frac{1}{2}$	$16\frac{1}{2}$	$17\frac{3}{4}$	$17\frac{3}{4}$	$17\frac{3}{4}$	$17\frac{3}{4}$	in.
EC	=	8	10	10.5	11	11.5	12	12.5	13	cm
		$3\frac{1}{4}$	4	4	$4\frac{1}{4}$	$4\frac{1}{2}$	$4\frac{3}{4}$	5	5	in.

6 Basic set-in-sleeve pattern, knitted in three colours changed at one-third and two-thirds of the total rows

5 Shoulder shaping should be worked by pushing several needles to holding position at the armhole edge on alternate rows, then knit one row over all needles. This gives a smooth line to sew up the seam, instead of the steps made by casting off along the shoulder.

6 Do not cast off any neck stitches – this will make the neckband tight. All shaping is done by pushing needles to holding position, and picking up the neckband stitches directly onto these stitches.

7 When knitting the neckband, place the end stitch from the back neck onto the same needle as the last stitch from the front neck. There is then a small overlap which allows for the stitching of the shoulder seam. If the shoulders are to be grafted, this overlap is not necessary as you will be making an extra stitch with the grafted seam, between the shoulders. At the neck edge pull the grafting stitch a little tighter to ease it into the neck.

BACK

Using WY cast on 108 114 121 127 135 141 147 155 sts. Knit about 10 rows (transfer every 3rd st to next needle for a mock rib). Knit 1 row with nylon cord.
Change to MT–3, knit 2 rows with sewing thread.
Change to MY, knit 18 rows.
Knit 1 row at tension 9.
Change to MT–2, knit 20 rows.
RC 41.
Fill empty needles and pick up sts from first row knitted in sewing thread.
RC 000.
Knit to RC 86 108 124 130 136 142 148 148.

Shape armhole
At beg of next 2 rows cast off 4 sts.
At beg of next 2 rows cast off 3 sts.
At beg of next 2 rows cast off 2 sts.
Dec 1 st at beg next 4 6 6 6 8 8 10 10 rows (64 84 91 97 101 105 109 113 sts).
Knit to RC 152 178 192 204 214 222 226 230.

Shape shoulders
Push 26 28 37 41 45 45 47 49 sts in centre to HP with all needles at right. Knit on left shoulder sts only. COL, knit 1 row.
Carr now at neck edge of knitting.
Push 4 6 6 6 7 7 7 needles opposite carr at

shoulder edge to HP on next 6 rows, wrapping inside needle.
Push all needles to UWP and knit 1 row. Take off onto WY, or cast off.
Knit other shoulder to match.
Take back neck sts off onto WY or garter bar.

FRONT

Knit as back to RC 130 152 162 174 184 192 196 200.

Shape front neck
Carr on right.
Leaving 21 32 37 38 40 42 45 45 sts in WP nearest to carr, push all others to HP, set carr to hold.
On every row, at neck edge push 1 needle to HP for 8 8 10 10 12 12 14 14 rows.
Hang a claw weight at neck edge of these sts, and knit straight to RC 152 178 192 204 214 222 226 230.
Shape shoulder as for back. Knit other side to match.
Leave 26 28 37 44 44 45 49 49 sts in centre in HP on the needles.
Do not remove from machine.

NECKBAND

Pick up sts evenly from both sides of front neck alongside needles in centre in HP. Pick up entire st at the edge, not just one thread of it. There should be about 60 64 70 70 72 72 76 78 sts from front neck (if you have a couple more or less than this it will not be significant enough to alter the size). On needles beside the front neck pick up 5 sts from the straight rows knitted at side of back neck, placing first one on same needle as front neck then replace all sts held on WY from back and 5 sts from the other side (approx 88 90 126 126 128 128 132 134 sts).
Transfer every 3rd st to next needle for mock rib.
RC 000.
Knit 12 rows, gradually reducing tension to MT–4. Knit loose fold row. Return to MT–4 and knit 12 rows gradually in c. to MT. Take off on WY.

SLEEVES

Using WY cast on 50 56 59 61 63 65 67 68 sts.
Make hem as back.
RC 000.

Increase 1 st at beg of next 2 rows and inc 1 st at beg of every 6th 7th, 7th 8th, 7th 8th, 6th 7th, 5th 6th, 5th 6th, 5th 6th, 5th 6th row to 82 88 91 95 103 107 109 115 sts.
Knit to RC 114 136 150 150 160 160 160 160.

Shape armhole
RC 000.
Cast off 4 4 5 5 5 6 6 6 sts at beg of next 2 rows.
Cast off 1 st at beg of every row for 21 24 34 34 38 40 42 44 rows.
Cast off 2 sts at beg of every row for 4 4 4 4 6 6 6 6 rows.
Cast off 3 sts at beg of every row for 0 0 0 4 4 4 6 6 6 rows.
Cast off remaining 24 24 31 31 31 31 35 sts.

TO MAKE UP
Stitch or graft the shoulders together.
Turn the neckband over and catch down through every stitch inside. Sew in the sleeves. Stitch the sleeve and side seams.
  Pull hems down well before joining the sides.

Cardigans and jackets

The basic block is used for these. Make the shape about 1 cm ($\frac{1}{2}$ in.) larger all round. This gives 2 cm ($\frac{3}{4}$ in.) extra ease as the garment is usually worn over others. If it is intended as a coat, then much more ease should be allowed so that it can be put on over clothes without a struggle. At least 10cm (4 in.) should be allowed above the normal size, more if you want a looser fitting style. Length is a matter for personal preference but a cardigan worn over a jumper looks better if it comes below the hem of the jumper, so about 1–3cm ($\frac{1}{2}$–1$\frac{1}{2}$ in.) should be added to the length.

  The front of the jumper block can be cut in half. There is no need to make any allowance for the front bands, as this small amount of extra width is in the place at the front of the body where it is needed.

  The small children's sizes in the basic pattern with set-in sleeves are shown as a cardigan (fig. 7). Adult sizes can be adapted by calculating the number of extra stitches and rows needed from your tension swatch, and knitted in the same way.

Sleeveless slipovers

The armhole is made larger in this style to accommodate the width of the armband. The basic block pattern is used and the armhole shaping is enlarged by 2 to 3cm (1–1$\frac{1}{4}$ in.) This means that the shoulder width is less, and the length from the bottom to the armhole shaping has fewer rows.

  This type of garment usually has a V-neck. These are dealt with in chapter 4. A lower curved neckline is also attractive. Draw this onto your block pattern. It is then a simple matter to calculate the rows and stitches from your tension swatch for the lower, wider neck.

Pattern for a basic children's cardigan

To fit	51	56	61	66	cm
	20	22	24	26	in.
Length	31	37	39	42	cm.
	12	14$\frac{1}{2}$	15$\frac{1}{2}$	16$\frac{1}{2}$	in.
Materials	150–180 gm 4-ply acrylic				
Tension	29 sts and 40 rows to 10cm (4 in.) at MT approx 7				

PATTERN NOTES

1 The body is made all in one piece. There are not enough needles to make the larger sizes like this, although it is possible to knit one front and the back together, thus having only one seam under the arm, up to size 86cm (34 in.) in stocking stitch.

2 The garment can be fitted with a zip instead of putting on button bands. Crochet rows of crab stitch along the front, or add one of the bands described in chapter 6.

3 To convert the cardigan pattern back to a jumper for children, knit two backs up to the row given for the neck shaping. Finish the shoulders in two halves like the cardigan.

BACK AND TWO FRONTS KNITTED TOGETHER
Using WY cast on 158 170 184 200 sts.
Knit a few rows (transfer every 3rd st to next needle for mock rib).
Knit 1 row with nylon cord.
RC 000.
Change to sewing cotton and MT–3. Knit 2 rows.

Change to MY and knit to RC 12 14 16 16.
Knit 1 loose row.
Return to MT−2 and knit 14 16 18 18 rows.
Fill empty needles.
Pick up first row knitted in cotton and make hem.
RC 000.
Change to MT and knit to RC 62 72 78 82. COR.

Shape armholes
Leaving 39 42 46 50 sts in WP next to carr, push all others to HP. Set carr to hold.
Left front:
Knit 1 row.
Cast off 4 sts at beg of next row. Knit 1 row.
Cast off 3 sts at beg of next row. Knit 1 row.
Continue to dec 1 st at armhole edge at beg alt rows to 29 32 36 40 sts.
Knit to RC 91 101 109 117.

Shape neck
Push 7 7 8 9 sts to HP at neck edge, opposite carr.
Hang a claw weight in centre to hold sts down.

Knit 1 row. Dec 1 st at neck edge by pushing needle to HP on next 8 8 9 9 rows.
Knit straight to RC 110 122 130 134 on remaining 14 17 19 22 sts.
Cast off sts straight across. On these small sizes with a few sts there is no need to slope the shoulders.
Take sts in HP at neck off onto WY.
Turn RC back to 62 72 78 82.
Take carriage to other side of needle bed and knit right front of the cardigan to match, reversing all shapings.

Back
Turn RC back to 62 72 78 82.
At beg of next 2 rows cast off 4 sts.
At beg of next 2 rows cast off 3 sts.
Cast off 1 st at beg of every row to 60 66 72 80 sts.
Continue to knit straight to RC 110 122 130 134.
Cast off 14 17 19 22 sts next to carr. Knit 1 row and cast off same number at other side.
Take neck sts off onto WY.

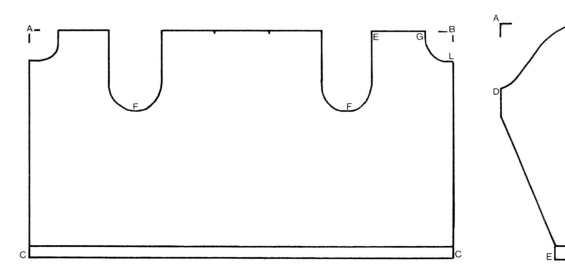

7 Children's all-in-one cardigan

Body						Sleeve					
AB =	56	60	65	67	cm	AB =	11	11	12	13	cm
	22	23½	25½	26½	in.		4¼	4¼	4¾	5	in.
AC =	26	29	31	33	cms	BC =	27	28	32	35	cm
	10¼	11½	12	13	in.		10½	11	12½	13¾	in.
FE =	29	29	31	35	cm	DE =	21	23	27	29	cm
	11½	11½	12	13¾	in.		8¼	9	10½	11½	in.
EG =	5	6	6	7	cm	EC =	6	7	8	9	cm
	2	2¼	2¼	2¾	in.		2¼	2¾	3¼	3½	in.
BL =	5	5	5	6	cm						
	2	2	2	2¼	in.						

SLEEVES

Cast on with WY 40 44 48 50 sts.

Transfer sts and knit hem as for bottom of back and fronts.

RC 000.

Inc 1 st at beg of next 2 rows and every 4th 5th, 5th 6th, 6th 7th, 7th 8th rows to 62 64 70 74 sts. Knit to RC 68 78 92 100.

Shape armhole

Cast off 5 5 6 6 sts at beg of next 2 rows. Dec 1 st at beg every row for 24 28 30 34 rows.

Cast off 2 sts at beg of next row for 8 rows (all sizes).

Cast off remaining 12 10 12 16 sts.

Sew shoulder seams and replace neck sts onto machine for neckband as follows:

From left front sts held on WY and about 5 6 6 6 sts from side of neck.

From back replace sts on WY, and same number from right front.

Total approx 74 93 100 106 sts.

Transfer every 3rd st to next needle for mock rib and change to MT−2.

Knit 10 rows, gradually decreasing tension to MT−4.

Knit 1 loose row for fold.

Knit 10 rows gradually increasing tension to MT−1.

Either take off onto WY and stitch down neckband, or pick up sts from 1st row in mock rib onto needles (there is no need to fill the empty needles).

Knit 1 row at MT + 1 and cast off loosely.

FRONT BANDS

Buttonhole band

Pick up along right front edge approx 76 84 92 96 sts.

*Knit 4 rows at MT−1. Transfer one st to next needle at equal intervals 5 6 8 8 times along the row. Leave needle in WP and knit 4 rows.**

Knit 1 loose row.

Repeat from * to **. Finish as for neckband. Sew round buttonholes through both layers of band.

Button band

Knit band onto left front, omitting buttonholes. Stitch buttons on to correspond with buttonholes.

Pockets

These can be added to any garment, but some planning is necessary before the fronts of the garment are knitted.

Make the pockets large enough. Measure the width across the hand, including the thumb, and the depth should not be less than that from the base of the thumb – about 15–18cm (6–7 in.) for an adult.

Patch pockets

The only pockets that can be added as an afterthought are patch pockets which are sewn to the garment after it is finished. These can be decorated with a motif or a textured pattern, but they must be stitched on carefully, making sure they are straight.

The neatest patch pocket is one which is attached to the front as it is knitted. This involves leaving a stitch out of work at each side where the pocket will fit – so you have to make a decision about where it will go first.

Mark the row where the bottom of the pocket will be by running a length of sewing thread in with the yarn as you knit. This can be pulled out later. Transfer the stitch each side to the next needle and continue to knit for the depth of the pocket. Pick up the stitch from the row below to fill the empty needles when you reach the top of the pocket and complete the front.

Hold the front upside-down with the bottom hem uppermost, right side facing. Pick up the stitches from the marked row onto the needles. Knit one row. At both ends of every row place the bar, made by the stitch out of work, onto the edge needle. Knit until all the bars are picked up and the pocket is attached neatly at each side. Continue to knit the welt straight on: 8–12 rows for the pocket top (transfer to mock rib if you wish), one fold row, and the same number for the other side. Take off on waste yarn and stitch down.

To make a patch pocket on the purl side of the knitting, pick up the first row of stitches with the front the right way up, hem at the bottom.

Insert pockets

Knit until the position for the top of the pocket is reached on the garment front. Place the needles at each side of the pocket into holding position and knit the welt. Knit the number of rows required for the double welt. If you have used a mock rib, bring all the needles on the pocket top into working position and knit two or three rows with waste yarn. Knit one row with nylon cord. Bring all the needles each side of the pocket into working position on the next two rows and finish knitting the front.

To knit the pocket bag, hold the front with the bottom uppermost, wrong side facing, and pick up the stitches in main yarn from above the nylon cord. Knit the length needed for the pocket. Do not cast off the bottom of the pocket but take it off on waste yarn. You can then stitch it down through every stitch, and up the sides. Pull out the nylon cord, and removing the waste yarn from the welt, stitch that into place.

Alternative neckband

A quick neckband which is knitted separately can be made by casting on – loosely, so that the neck will not be tight – the required number of stitches to fit the neck. Knit the double band, reducing the tension towards the middle then pick up the first row of stitches in the main yarn onto the same needles. Knit one row across both sets of stitches.

Pick up the neck of the garment, wrong side facing, onto the needles, knit one loose row at tension 10, and cast off loosely. This gives a line of stitches on the right side which are purl and not knit, and looks similar to a back-stitched row of stitches. This purled row separates the neckband from the rest of the garment if both are knitted in stocking stitch. (This is used on the children's 'cat' design described in chapter 7.)

8 Neckband knitted separately and then picked up onto the neck with the right side facing to give a decorative row of purled stitches

Collars

These are not easy to make with the single bed, since an edging of some sort must be put round them to prevent them from curling.

Collars can be edged as follows:

1 *Crochet edging* Two rows of double crotchet will hold the edge flat.

2 *Braid* This can be sewn on afterwards.

3 *With a small hem* This can be added to the edge. Cast on four extra stitches at each side of the needles for the collar width at the outside edge. For four rows decrease one stitch at both ends of each row. For the next four rows increase one stitch at the beginning of each row. This will give a mitred corner, and four rows across the bottom and four stitches up the sides of the collar to turn under. Stitch down afterwards. Decrease within the four hem stitches to the number required for neck edge.

To make a lined collar

A matching or toning finer yarn is preferable for the undercollar, or it will be very bulky. The stitches can be picked up from round the neck of the garment to knit the underhalf of the collar. Pick up the stitches with the wrong side of the knitting facing. Thread up with finer yarn and knit at main tension the depth of the collar (decided from the tension square). Increase stitches at each side at regular intervals to make the collar about 5cm (2 in.) wider at the fold. (You may want to make more increases for a wider collar.) Change to the main yarn and continue to knit the top of the collar, decreasing the stitches. Keep the same tension for both yarns. If the finer yarn seems flimsy it will not matter very much since it will be hidden under the collar. It is only being knitted to hold the edge of the collar flat. Take off on waste yarn. The stitches can be sewn down on the inside of the collar to cover the picked-up edge. Interfacing can be used to make a firmer collar if desired, for a jacket for example. Sew up the sides of the collar and press.

Notes on making up

Grafting

The shoulder seams are best grafted together to give a neat finish. In fact, if it is done well the seam is quite invisible. When grafting, another row of stitches is made between the open loops of the two rows being joined.

Place the two shoulder edges to be joined edge to edge, knit side up. To begin with it is perhaps easier to unravel the waste yarn a few stitches at a time from each side, so that you can see which is the actual stitch. With practice you will be able to do this with the waste yarn in position and there is less risk of the stitches running down. Press the knitting lightly – this will set the stitches in place so that they do not escape so easily.

Thread a tapestry needle with the end of the yarn from one side. Take it up through the end stitch and across to the other piece of knitting, down into the first stitch and up through the second, across back to the first side and down into the first stitch again and up through the second. You will see that you have made the shape of a knitted stitch between the two pieces of knitting. Continue to do this across the shoulder, going into every stitch twice. Try to make the stitches the same size as the original knitted stitches and do not pull them too tight.

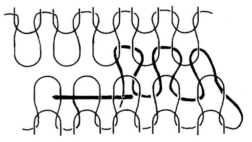

9 Grafting. The open loops on each side are joined by making another row of stitches with the needles

Mattress stitch (or ladder stitch)

This is by far the neatest way of joining seams by hand. The stitches match exactly on the right side, whether that is the knit or purl side of the work. It is not perfectly flat, as one stitch from each side is taken in on the reverse. The seam is made with the right side of the work facing. Insert the needle into the space between the first and second stitches and bring it up again one or two bars further up. Take it across to the other piece and put it into the same place between the stitches. This zigzag stitch can be done loosely for a few stitches, then by pulling the thread tight the two pieces will close up together and the seam will be invisible. This is the best way to sew up where patterns or stripes have to be matched.

If a flatter seam is required, instead of stitching between the stitches, take the needle into the centre of the first stitch and bring it up in the centre of the one above so that there is only a half-stitch seam inside.

Seams can also be joined using a sewing machine. More details on this are given in chapter 7, together with cut-and-sew.

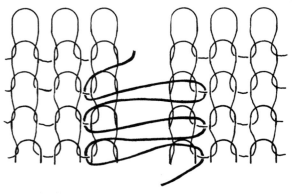

10 Mattress stitch. With the right side facing, take the thread under the bar between the stitches on each side. Pull the thread tight and the seam will close

Joining open stitches onto rows

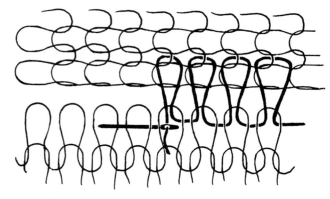

11 Joining open stitches onto rows. Take the thread under the bar for mattress stitch and twice into the open-stitch loops

If attaching open loops of stitches onto the rows at the side of the knitting, for example when joining a set-in sleeve to the back/front, a very neat seam is made by sewing it on with a mixture of grafting and mattress stitch. Insert the needle under the bar between the first and second stitches of the rows of knitting and take it down into the first open loop of the stitches of the sleeve. Come up through the second loop and into the place where the stitch came out on the rows. Go into each stitch and into the same place on the rows twice.

Casting off

1 Take the first stitch on the right and place it into the next needle, taking it round the back of the sinker pin instead of in front. This means that it is held out in the position in which it was knitted, so the cast-off row does not pull tight. Continue along the row like this. It is not necessary to take every stitch round behind the sinker pins so long as most of them are taken this way. This method of casting off can be used anywhere on the garment. It has the advantage that the weight of the knitting is held on the machine and not dragging down. When completed, lift the knitting off the sinker pins.

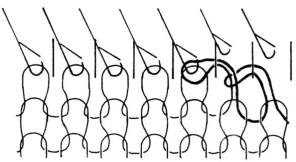

12 Casting off round the sinker pins to keep the stitches spread to the width as they were knitted

2 *Using the latch tool* With practice this can become a very quick way to cast off, but the stitches of the last row must be knitted very loosely, or the cast-off will produce a very tight edge. By the time you are halfway across, the stitches may be so tight that you cannot latch them together. This is not suitable for casting off a few stitches such as at an underarm shaping because these few stitches cannot be knitted loosely without distorting the whole row.

If you are using a fine yarn and the main tension is a very small number, e.g. 2 or 3, then by knitting the last row at tension 10 the stitches will be loose enough to latch off, but if the main tension is about 7 or larger the stitch will not be big enough. To get a large stitch on the last row it must be knitted by hand. Place your straight-sided needle pusher at the back of the needle bed (on most models it has a groove on it which fits over the ridge at the back of the bed) and taking the yarn over the needle by hand, knit the stitch back until the needle butt touches the flat edge of the pusher. This ensures even larger stitches along the row.

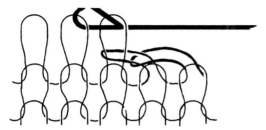

13 Casting off with the latch tool along a row of very loose stitches

3 *Using a linker* Brother and Knitmaster have now produced a 'casting-off machine'. It can also be used to join seams together and so is called a linker, but all it does is cast off by the latch tool method automatically. Follow the instructions exactly as they are given in the instruction book. When all the needles are forward to D or E position, pull the stitches slightly forward, though *not* over the latches. This prevents the stitch from being trapped against the sinkers, if any needles are not quite straight, and the machine latch needle can pick it up more easily. Hang a claw weight at the right-hand edge of the knitting so that the cast-off stitches fall away and the stitches are firmly held into the hooks.

Dropped shoulders

This has become a very popular style over recent years, partly because it cuts out the shaping at the armhole and sleeve head, and partly because all-over patterns look better without the interruption of the armhole seams.

The body is knitted straight to the shoulder, but in order to have sufficient ease where the sleeve joins the body, the position for the armhole is lowered. The sleeve must therefore be knitted wider at the top. If the sleeve is made the same

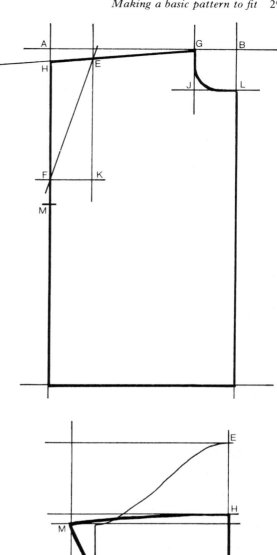

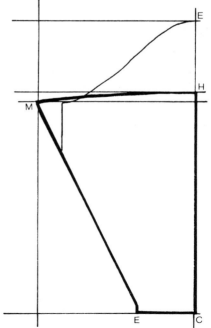

14 Dropped shoulder block, showing the construction lines

width as the basic block it will feel tight under the arm. The rounded top of the sleeve has been lost so it will be more comfortable, and hang over the shoulder better, if the centre of the sleeve top is curved. This is done by putting some needles to holding position at each side, so that more rows are knitted on the centre stitches. If the sleeve is very wide, like a dolman or batwing, then this curve at the top is not so necessary.

Batwing sleeves

The design for a very low-fitting sleeve should be worked out without allowing any ease on the circumference of the body. The wide armhole will give all the ease on the garment that is required. Use the basic block as the starting point of the design. The style can be knitted in several ways.

1 *All in one piece, knitted from cuff to cuff* Cast on the number of stitches at the cuff and increase evenly for the length of the underarm seam, to give the width of sleeve required. This could be to the maximum width of the needle bed. Do not make this full sleeve too long or the fullness will hang over the hand. Calculate the exact length needed.

There are not enough needles to knit across the back and front together (some exceptions to this are if it is a small size being made, or if using a tuck stitch which has made the work very wide). At the top of the sleeve all the stitches are removed in two halves, onto waste yarn. Replace the stitches from one half of the sleeve onto the needles, leaving enough needles at the bottom edge to cast on the length needed for the front/back body. Knit the width of the body, cast off the same number of stitches at the bottom as were cast on and take the rest off onto waste yarn. Repeat with the other half of the stitches from the sleeve.

Put all the stitches on waste yarn onto the needles and knit the second sleeve down to the cuff.

The front and back can be knitted vertically, from hem to neck, and the sleeve sewn onto the sides. Welts are picked up from the bottom edges and knitted afterwards.

2 *Knitting a batwing sideways in two halves* Cast on half the number of stitches needed for the cuff

and knit the sleeve by making more frequent increases at the underarm side of the sleeve, and more gradual increases at the other side to follow the extended shoulder slope. Knit across the body. Neck shaping can be done sideways or cut-and-sew can be used for speed. The sloping shoulder and upper edge of the sleeve will give a comfortable fit and the armhole curve will not be missed.

3 *Knitted vertically in two pieces* Cast on half the number of stitches needed for the front to one side of the needle bed and increase one stitch at the side until the full length of the sleeve is reached. Knit half the width of the cuff then shape the upper edge of the sleeve and shoulder by putting needles to holding position in section on each row, beginning at the cuff end, until the full length of the jumper has been knitted to the neck. Continue to knit downwards on the back, bringing needles gradually back to working position, and knit for the full width of the cuff. Decrease at the underarm until the bottom edge is reached and finish the hem.

Knit another piece the same, reversing the shaping. These can be mattress-stitched together up the centre. This seam will be a very neat join, but each half of the garment could have a different colour or pattern on it to accentuate the two halves. The seam then does not matter so much even if it is not at all obvious.

The neck can be shaped as you knit in the usual way, by using holding position, but as soon as the shaping is complete take the stitches off onto waste yarn. These same needles will be needed to cast on again for the back neck.

When increasing on every row – that is, at both ends next to and opposite the carriage – the usual way is to lift a stitch from the row below onto the needle at the side opposite the carriage. This is fine for two or three rows but it does make the edge rather tight, so when increasing for a batwing sleeve the easiest way is to use a spare length of matching yarn. Bring the needle forward and e-wrap it with the spare yarn. Knit the row. Bring the next needle forward and knit the row. Carry the spare yarn up the side of the knitting and e-wrap the next end stitch. Continue to do this for the sleeve side. The edge will not be pulled tight and the small lengths of yarn will be sewn into the seam when the garment is finished.

When decreasing at the edge on every row, the edge will pull tight unless a claw weight is hung on the knitting. Move it up every few rows and as you knit the end stitch will be made a little larger. If it still seems tight, a length of spare yarn can be used to knit an extra stitch as you decrease, but do not do this on every row, only on alternate rows as before. Place the stitch onto the next needle to decrease, then knit the two stitches with the spare yarn. This will give extra length to the side stitches.

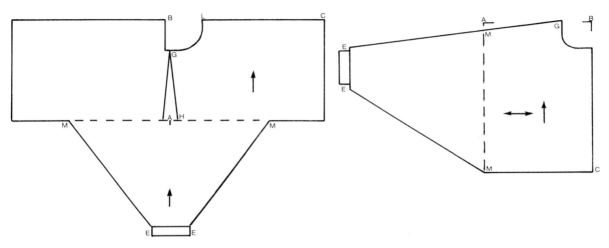

15 Batwing styles. *Top* Knitted from cuff to cuff, all pieces joined on the machine. *Bottom* Garment knitted in two halves, either from the bottom up over the shoulder and down the back, or from cuff to cuff with a seam along the top of the sleeve

CHAPTER 3

Three-dimensional shapes

All garments are made to fit a three-dimensional shape but most are actually knitted in only two dimensions, as flat pieces, and sewn together. It is possible to knit some items shaped on the machine, and this is done by partial knitting.

It is used for shaping a garment when more rows of knitting are required in one place than another – in order to make a curve, a bump, a fold or simply to hold stitches not being knitted until required. It is usually done by using the holding position; needles are brought forward as far as they will go, to D or E position, and the lever or button on the carriage is set to hold so that they will not knit. All other needles will knit normally.

When several needles are to be put into holding position at the end of a row, they must be pushed forward at the end opposite the carriage. Otherwise a long float of yarn will be taken across the knitting before the carriage gets to the needles to be knitted. If only one needle is to be put into holding position then it can be done at either end of the bed.

A small gap will occur in the knitting at the end of each set of stitches in holding position. Sometimes these small holes can be used as a design feature, for example at the corners of a lacy shawl, or used for threading ribbon or cord, but usually they are not desirable. In order to prevent these holes the rows must be joined together, and this can be done in two ways.

1 The inside needle in holding position nearest to the carriage should have the yarn looped round it before knitting the next row. Use this method when the stitches are to be put onto waste yarn and replaced on the needles. By wrapping the yarn right round the needle a larger loop is made which is easier to pick up again with the stitch.

2 *Automatic wrap* If only one needle is to be brought out to holding position then it can be brought forward at the side *nearest* to the carriage, and as the next row is knitted the yarn will automatically wrap round the needle to prevent the hole. If the stitches are not to be picked up again this is a quick method, but there is a tighter loop over the needle. When shaping segments of several needles in holding position, such as when knitting a flared skirt, then all the needles in the block can be brought out to holding position at the end opposite the carriage. Knit the row and bring one more needle out next to the carriage to make the automatic wrap.

The same rules apply for returning the stitches to working position. If several needles together are pushed back they must be at the side opposite to the carriage and the yarn wrapped round the inside needle. A single needle can be taken back either next to the carriage (automatic wrap) or at the opposite end and manually wrapped. The stitches will knit if taken back only to the upper working position. Take care not to push them back too far or the stitches will come off the needle over the latch.

Stitches being knitted must be weighted down in some way because with needles in holding position the knitting does not drop down. Stitches tend to ride up on the needles and may be pushed off. Hang one of the claw weights onto the work, moving it up every few rows.

When part of the work is in holding position, the brushes under the sinker plate rub along the

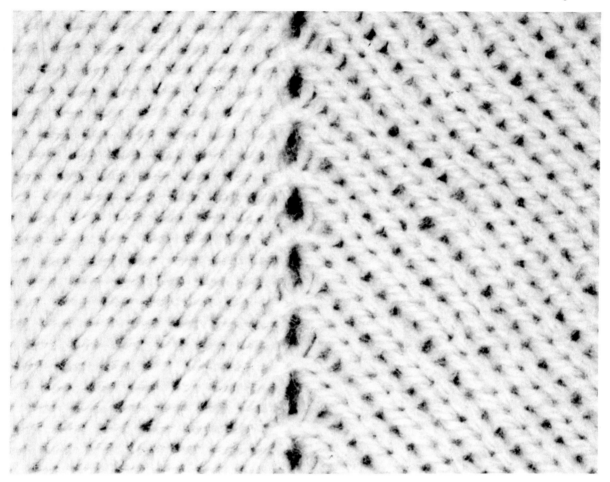

16 The holes made between the rows by not wrapping needles in holding position

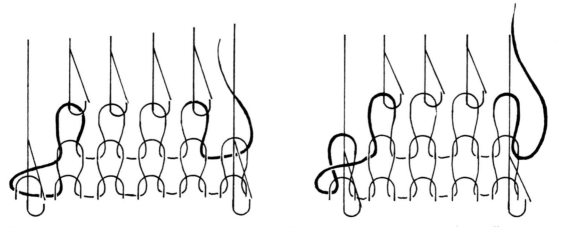

17 The manual wrapping of needles in holding position (*left*) makes a longer loop over the needle to pick up again. A tighter loop is made by using the automatic wrap (*right*)

knitting hanging below the needles. This will not affect the knitting for two or three rows, but if many rows are knitted then the brushes will fluff up the fabric through continually passing over the same stitches. If the purl side is to be the wrong side then it will not matter very much, but if the purl side is the right side, for example when knitting in tuck stitch, or weaving, then this brushed area will spoil the garment. To avoid this happening, the stitches below the bed should be covered. Sometimes a piece of Sellotape stuck over them will do, but this can catch and come off on the sinker plate. The best method is to hang a piece of an old tension square onto the sinker pins which protrude between the needles. The brushes will then rub on this and not on the knitting, and it is quickly and easily removed.

Most of the usual reasons for using the holding position when knitting are explained in the individual designs, such as for shaping a neckline, sloping a shoulder or curving the hem of a skirt. Quite complicated, three-dimensional shapes can be worked out using partial knitting, simply by thinking about which area of the knitting needs more rows than another. The following patterns can only be made in this way.

Hat with a brim

This is knitted sideways all in one piece. Since one of the characteristics of knitwear is that it is elastic, this is taken into consideration when making the brim. However, to avoid a lot of strain on the stitches, the brim is shaped so that more rows are knitted around the outside edge than near the head. Also the knitting needs to turn under the brim, so a small facing of straight knitting, with the same number of rows as the head part, is left to be stitched up inside the crown of the hat.

Materials	45 gm 1-strand bouclé 2-ply + 1 strand 2/30 knitted together, or a fine 4-ply
Tension	30 sts and 42 rows to 10cm (4 in.) at MT approx 7

PATTERN NOTES

1 This hat will fit an adult head measuring 56–61cm (22–24 in.) in circumference. For a larger or looser fit, increase the tension by one or two dots. This will make the stitch bigger in both directions so the crown of the hat will be larger. A smaller hat may be made by decreasing the tension a little.

2 Do not cast on in the usual way with equal numbers of stitches each side of 0. Use the numbered needles to the right and left of 0. Then the shaping is easier to see – one has only to look at the numbers on the needle bed to see which needles are to be in HP.

Cast on 45 sts to left of 0 and 20 to right, using WY.
Knit a few rows ending with COL.
RC 000.
Change to MY and MT. Knit 1 row. COR.
At left edge (crown of hat) put 6 needles to HP. Set carr to hold.
Knit 1 row, bring 1 needle next to carriage to HP, (automatic wrap; needle number 38). Knit 1 row.
Bring 4 needles to HP at left. Knit 1 row.
Bring 1 needle to HP next to carr (number 33). Knit 1 row.
Bring all needles up to number 10 at left to HP. Knit the row.
Bring 1 needle to HP next to carr and 5 needles to HP at right. Knit the row.
COR. RC 6.
The 5 needles on the right are the sts for the facing of the brim, the same number of rows required here as for the crown.
Continue to knit on remaining needles in WP and shape brim by bringing 1 needle near carr to HP and 4 opposite carr on every row until there are only 2 needles left in WP. COR.
Return all needles at left to UWP so that they will knit back. Knit 1 row.
Return all needles at right to UWP. Knit 1 row.
RC 12.
All needles are now knitting.
Repeat this sequence of 12 rows 31 times more. RC 348.
Take off onto WY, and graft edges together.
Run a thread through the stitches at the crown and gather them in, sewing up the small hole at the centre.

TO MAKE UP
The stiffening for the brim is made by drawing

18 Hat with a brim knitted sideways in one piece. Brim shaped by holding position

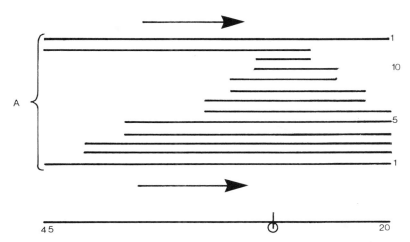

19 Diagram of the needles knitting for one section of the brimmed hat. A = one complete repeat of the shaping sequence, crown of hat to the left, brim to the right. This could be drawn onto the electronic pattern sheet and knitted using slip stitch

two circles. The inside one is 19cm (7½ in.) in diameter, the outer one 20cm (11½ in.) in diameter, to give a 5-cm (2-in.) brim. Use this pattern to cut out the stiffening material. Two layers of medium-weight Vilene give a firm but not too stiff brim.

Tack the stiffening materials inside the shaped piece of the brim. The straight edge of five stitches' width is sewn up inside the crown of the hat. A row of stitching near to the edge of the brim and another next to the crown can be done on the sewing machine, or small running stitches by hand. This will keep the stiffening in place.

A band round the outside of the hat can be made by plaiting three cords made on the machine, or a knitted braid. Cords are made as follows:

Cast on 3 to 5 sts (depending on the thickness required).
Knit 2 rows, RC MT − 2 and set carriage to slip in one direction only. All needles will knit on one pass of carriage, and none will knit on return. Hold tail of yarn down below knitting and two edges of the knitting will curve towards one another and join to make a tube.
Knit for the length required. Tension needs to be reduced because slack yarn across knitting will be taken up by sts as they are pulled down.
A flat braid to go round the hat can be made using tuck stitch:
Bring forward 7 sts to WP, push 3 and 5 (each side of the centre needle) back, and cast on over 5 remaining needles. Knit 4 rows.
Pull centre stitch forward to holding position, set carriage to hold and knit 4 rows. Push needle back to UWP, knit 4 rows. Repeat last 8 rows until braid is long enough to go round the hat.

Beret

In order to make the circular shape, fewer stitches are needed at the centre than at the outside edge. A beret has a section around the edge which folds underneath, so this also needs fewer rows than the extreme edge. Like the hat the beret is knitted sideways. It is made up of ten segments, which will make the complete circle, and each segment can be knitted in a different colour or a thin line can be knitted between the sections in a different

colour. This pattern is to fit an average adult head, but one for a child could be knitted by reducing the number of stitches needed for the crown − estimated from a tension swatch − and the shaping knitted in exactly the same way. The measurement needed is from the brow to the centre of the head. The 50 stitches cast on for the adult size is only half the finished width.

Materials   For a beret all in one colour, 40gm 4-ply equivalent yarn

Tension   24 sts and 40 rows to 10cm (4 in.) MT approx 6

Using WY cast on 50 sts. Knit a few rows.
Change to MY and MT knit 2 rows.
To shape top of crown, push 1 needle to HP on *every* row at left. This will automatically wrap the end needle. At the same time when carr is at left, push 13 needles at right to HP, knit 1 row and bring 1 needle to HP next to carr.
Knit 1 row, COL.
Before knitting next row push needles in HP at right to UWP so that they knit back on the next row.
Repeat this sequence until there are only 2 sts in HP above 14-st fold line at right. Push all needles at left to UWP and knit 1 row. Push needles at right to UWP and knit across all needles.
This has knitted one segment of the beret. Knit 9 more.
Take off on WY and graft the seam.

The instructions sound complicated but study fig. 20 and remember that you are knitting one less stitch at the left on every row, and only two out of four rows on the 14 stitches at the right. Every time the carriage is on the left when all needles at the right are knitting then you must push 13 forward; if there are 14 needles already in HP then you must push them back.

TO MAKE UP
The top of the beret can be drawn up with a thread, but the small hole in the crown can be filled with a loop of cord − knit about 20 rows and sew into position, unravelling any extra rows after stitching − or covered with a button, or make a pompon to finish the top. Turn in four rows of knitting at inside edge and stitch down the small hem.

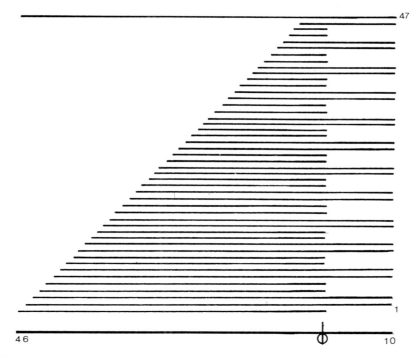

47

1

46

10

20 Diagram to show one complete section of the beret, crown to the left and the turned-under edging to the right

Gloves

Gloves are included in this chapter because they are a three-dimensional shape which many people find confusing to knit flat on the machine.

Measurements	To fit average adult hand
Materials	50gm 4-ply yarn (three strands of 2/30 4-ply wool-and-nylon mixture)
Tension	25 sts and 38 rows to 10cm (4 in.) at MT approx 7

PATTERN NOTES

1 The first finger to be knitted must be the fourth finger which is in the centre of the needle bed and the centre of the glove.

2 The elastic quality of knitted fabric is taken into consideration when knitting the thumb. There is no need to knit a gusset !eading up to the actual thumb. The stitches are picked up from the palm of the glove since the thumb comes forward and not from the side of the hand.

LEFT-HAND GLOVE
Cast on 58 sts using WY. Knit a few rows and change to MY. Transfer the sts for a 2 × 1 mock rib, and set tension at MT − 2.
Knit 30 rows. Knit 1 loose row.
Change to MT and knit 30 rows.
Pick up 1st row of sts in MY and replace them on the needles, filling empty needles with a stitch to avoid a row of holes. If the line of the hem shows on the gloves it does not detract from the appearance as does a bad hem at the bottom of a garment.
Knit 20–30 rows, depending on how long you want the glove.
COR.
At the left side pull 12 needles forward so that sts are behind latches, and knit these back by hand using WY in a contrast colour. These are the stitches for the thumb.
Continue to knit across all needles for a further 14 rows.
Push 14 sts in centre to HP, set carr to hold, and knit all other sts onto WY. Push empty needles to NWP and set to knit needles back to WP.

4th finger

Each side of centre pick up next st from row below onto adjacent needles (16 sts in all).

Knit 26 rows. Do not cast off, but thread yarn through sts and remove from machine. Draw up top of finger, and sew up finger seam.

3rd finger

On centre needles, pick up 2 sts from base of 4th finger. Pick up 7 sts at each side from those taken off onto WY. Cast on 1 st at each end of next row (18 sts). Knit 30 rows. Take sts off as for 4th finger.

2nd finger

Pick up 2 sts in centre from base of 3rd finger,

pick up 8 sts each side of them from WY, cast on 1 each side (20 sts). Knit 35 rows. Take off sts as for 4th finger.

1st finger

As 3rd finger.

Thumb

Remove yarn from 12 sts knitted on hand and open out knitting – carefully so that sts do not unravel – into a straight line and pick up from the row below WY and from row above it (24 sts). Knit 24 rows. Take off and gather top like fingers.

RIGHT-HAND GLOVE

Make the thumb opening on the opposite side of the hand. Otherwise you will have two left gloves, and have to knit two more (right) gloves to make up the pairs – an easy mistake to make.

If you wish to put a Fair Isle pattern on the hand part of the glove, choose a design which has very short floats – otherwise the fingers will catch in them. Alternating needles knitted in different colours can be enough pattern for gloves. The floats are almost non-existent and it makes the hand part of the glove thicker and warmer.

A motif on the back of the hand only can be made, but this means that the hand section must be knitted in two halves.

After knitting the welt, take half the stitches off onto waste yarn, increase one stitch each side and knit the back of the hand with the pattern on it. Decrease one stitch each side and put the stitches to holding position. Knit the palm of the hand in stocking stitch, increasing one stitch each side. Turn the row counter back to the number above the welt and make the slit with waste yarn for the thumb. Knit to top. Decrease one stitch each side and knit one row across all needles. Continue as before to knit fingers. Extra stitches each side are used in sewing up the seams.

Partial knitting using a punchcard

Squares and spiral shapes can be made by using a punchcard. The carriage is set to slip, and as only the needles selected by the holes will knit, the others are held as if the holding cams on the carriage had been set. The needles cannot be wrapped so there is always a row of holes along

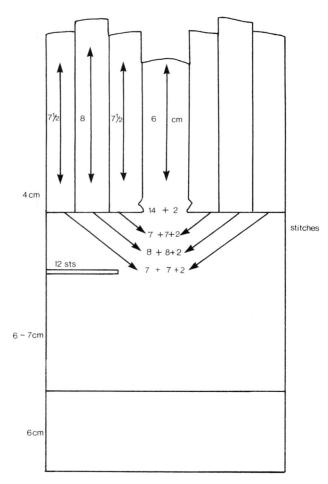

21 Glove. This is the right-hand glove flattened out, smallest finger in the centre, showing the number of stitches taken from each side for the fingers plus the extra two stitches cast on, one at each side

the shaped pieces. Always elongate these cards, as two rows must be knitted between shapings.

Using the punchcard in fig. 22, a flat square is produced with mitred corners. By knitting extra rows between the shaped areas, this card can be used for the edging of a square shawl, or as a yoke for a baby's matinee coat. Flat squares could be sewn together for blankets or cushion covers – knit in stripes or work each quarter in a different colour. If the card is marked out using only half the needles, a mirror-image of the design can be punched out alongside this one. The hole pattern will be a complete triangle on the card. A double-sided square will be knitted, which could be padded. Several sewn together would make a cot quilt.

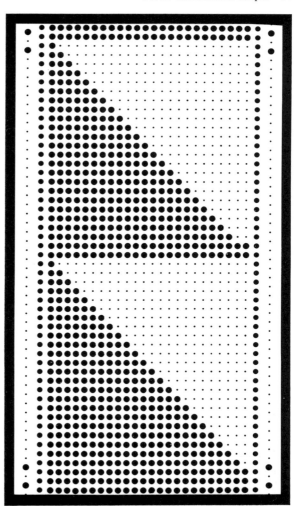

23 Punchcard used to knit a spiral. Knit five sections to complete the circle. Elongate the card and set the carriage to slip

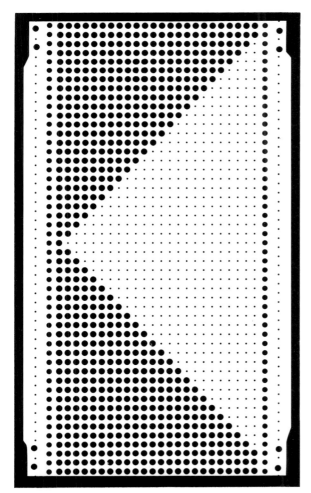

22 Punchcard for knitting a mitred corner. Elongate the card so that every row knits twice. Set to slip

The punchcard in fig. 23 will create a pentagon with a spiral pattern of holes where the shaping is made. This could also be knitted with extra rows between the shapings for a collar or frill for a cuff. By elongating the card even more so that several rows are knitted before the next slipped needle, a half-spherical shape is produced. Using only half the needles and a mirror-image of the pattern as above, a complete sphere can be made.

The disadvantage of using a punchcard is that the shape made is limited to a 24-stitch radius, which may not be large enough for many projects. The electronic machine, however, can produce a pattern up to 120 stitches wide, so the sheet could be marked in this way to knit a square or circle up to 240 stitches across. The spiral shape can be used on the electronic sheet to knit a flared skirt. Extra needles required for the length can be added at each end of the skirt and straight sections can be knitted between the shaping, as on the pleated skirt pattern (chapter 5).

Partial knitting of individual lengths of the row can produce a textured pattern. This may be rather slow to knit as a complete garment, but could be mixed with other stitches. Divide the row into equal lengths, about 10 or 12 stitches each. Begin at one end and push all needles except the first section to holding position. Knit on these needles, pushing one to holding position either next to the carriage (wrapping the needle) or opposite the carriage and leaving the needle unwrapped to make a decorative hole. Continue until only one needle remains in working position.

Push half the needles back so that they will knit. On the next row push the other half back and also the needles for the second section. Push first set to holding position, and knit on second set.

This kind of patterning could also be knitted using a punchcard. Punch out the card as for the mitred corner but using only 12 needles and the mirror-image of the shape, as if you are going to knit a double-sided square. It is just one corner that you repeat across the row. Divide the work into sections of 24 stitches, and set all but one section to holding position as before. Set the carriage to hold and also to slip. Knit the shaping on each section in turn across the row.

Any design using partial knitting which can fit into 24 stitches – or however wide the punchcard is – can be knitted using the card. It is worthwhile doing if it is a process which you will repeat several times.

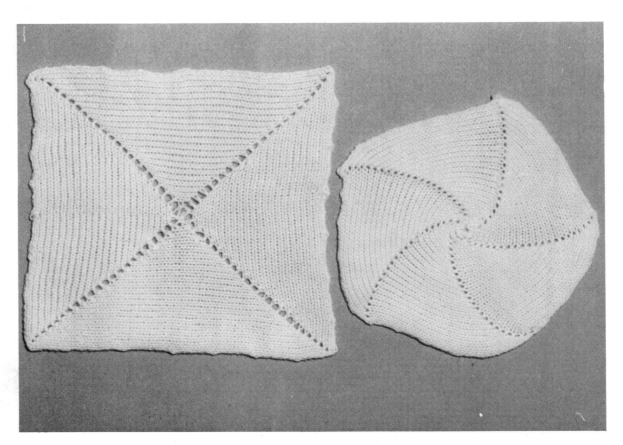

24 *Left* Mitred square   *Right* Spiral pentagon knitted using the punchcards. The end needles cannot be wrapped when using slip stitch so a row of holes is made along each section

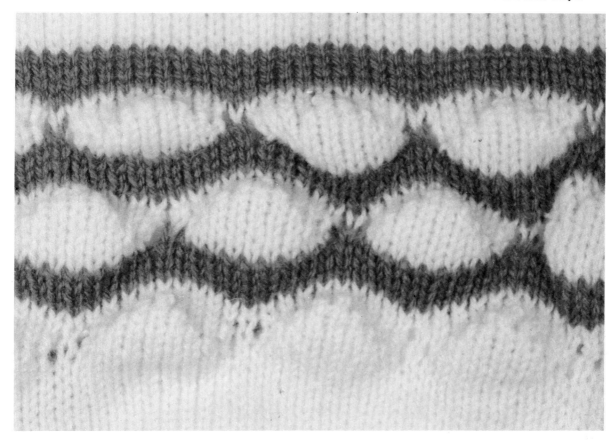

25 Knobbly pattern made by knitting extra rows on individual sections of each row. Contrast colour knitted between to accentuate the pattern made

Socks

This pattern is for short socks, so there is no shaping on the leg section. If you want to make knee socks (or over-knee socks) then the number of stitches needed round the top, either at calf or thigh, must be calculated from the tension square, and the number of rows needed for the length estimated in the same way. The stitches will need to be decreased into the ankle and the rate of decrease can be calculated by dividing the number of stitches to be decreased into the number of rows knitted.

For example:
Stitches needed round calf   84
Stitches needed at ankle   48
Number to be decreased   36 stitches, 18 each
                              side

Number of rows   130 rows
                              $130 \div 18 = 7$ with
                              remainder of 4

Decrease both ends of every seventh row and knit four rows straight at the ankle. The pattern fits a medium-sized foot.

The heel and toe shapings are done by using the punchcard and setting the carriage to slip, and the side foot seam is joined as you knit on the machine, so the socks are quickly finished. If you wish to make them longer or shorter then the number of rows knitted can be adjusted. If you want them wider then you will have extra needles each side of the punchcard at the heel shaping.

Bring one needle to holding position at the beginning of every row until there are 24 needles left in the centre. The punchcard can be engaged and the carriage also set to slip. Finish the shaping with the punchcard, and then return the holding position needles to upper working position so that they will knit back on each row until all are knitted.

If you want a narrower foot then you can start the heel and toe shaping further up the punchcard. For example if you have 20 needles to shape the toe, insert the punchcard at the row which shows 20 holes punched, click it round in the machine the number of times required to set that row as the first selecting row, and continue the shaping from there until all needles are knitting again.

Use a fairly thick yarn for hard-wearing boot socks. With a leather sole they make warm slippers.

Welly socks

To fit   19–24cm (7½–9½ in.) foot

Materials   Approx 50gm lightweight double knitting or a wool-and-nylon 4-ply, or 4 strands of 2/30

Tension   24 sts and 36 rows to 10cm (4 in.) MT approx 10

FIRST SOCK
Bring forward 48 needles to WP, over two full sections of patterning needles; that is, 12 needles to right of centre 0 and 36 needles to left of 0.
Push every 4th needle back to NWP for mock rib.
Using WY cast on and knit a few rows.
Change to MY and MT–2.
Knit 40 rows.
Knit 1 loose row.
At MT − 1 knit 40 rows.
Pick up first row of sts in MY filling empty needles.
RC 000.
Knit 40 rows.
Take half sts off on WY, and knit on remaining 24 needles.
Knit 50 rows.

Shape toe
Insert punchcard and lock on row 1.
Knit 1 row, set carr to slip and release card.
Continue until all needles are knitting again.
RC 118.

At both ends of every row pick up a loop from the side of the top foot section onto end needles, starting with edge sts of rows nearest to toe shaping. This joins upper and lower halves of the foot as you knit.
Knit to RC 168.

Shape heel
Re-set punchcard to row 1 and lock it.
Knit shaping as toe.
RC 186.
Take all sts off onto WY.
Graft both sets of sts on WY together, and sew side leg seam.

SECOND SOCK
Knit one extra row at the end of the leg so that the foot is knitted on the opposite half of the needles. The leg seam will then be on the inside of each sock.

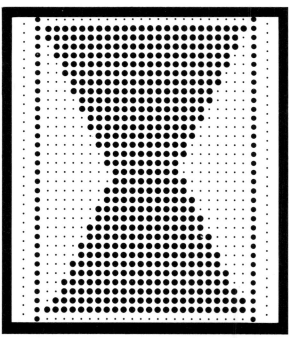

26 Punchcard used to decrease each side to turn the heel of a sock. Set the carriage to slip. Do not elongate this card, as it is punched out to knit every row

CHAPTER 4

V-necks and raglans

V-necks

The division of the knitting for a V-neck usually starts level with the beginning of the armhole, so for a raglan-sleeve sweater the V will be a little lower than for a set-in-sleeve jumper. The neckline can be started lower than this if desired. The number of rows knitted between the decreases at the neck edge will be greater, but the width of the neck stays the same. For example, worked out from a tension swatch, the depth of the neck is 24cm (9½ in.) or 100 rows, and the total width of the neck is 50 stitches or 15 cm (6 in.), so it will be necessary to decrease one stitch every fourth row up the neck edge (for a 4-ply garment this is the average rate of decrease). However, if the depth of the neck is increased to 32cm (12½ in.) or 128 rows, then the decreases must be made every five rows. The extra three rows can be worked straight at the shoulder.

There is a known number of stitches from the back neck and the tops of the raglans (if applicable), but the number for the sloping edge of the front neck is not known. The most accurate way of working this out is to measure the front slope and pick up the number of stitches for that measurement per 2.5cm (1 in.). For example, if on the tension swatch – worked in whatever yarn you wish – there are 7 stitches for every 2.5cm (1 in.), and the front measures 25cm (10 in.), then 70 stitches are required for the front. The band should be knitted one whole number tighter than the main tension. It will then make a firmer edge. If you have a charter you can measure the front of the V with the stitch rule, which will tell you immediately how many stitches are required. The

ruler not only tells you how many stitches to cast on for the main part of the garment but at any other place on the garment where stitches are to be picked up and knitted for bands. Although bands are knitted at a slightly tighter tension than the main knitting, the number of stitches is still assessed by using the original tension swatch.

The front neck can be judged by holding it up to the machine *slightly* stretched. This is only a rough estimate, but with experience you will be able to guess the number of stitches quite accurately.

If you do not want to make a mitre on a true rib band, it can be knitted as a straight piece and the ends crossed at the point of the V. There are only two layers of knitting, but for a single bed band which must be knitted double, the four layers at the V are rather bulky, so it is more important to shape the mitre of the V-neck band as you knit it.

Perhaps the easiest method is to put all stitches from one side of the V-neck (include the top of one sleeve for the raglan style) and the back neck onto the machine. Replace back neck and sleeve first, pull forward all needles required for the front and loop a few stitches at each end onto the needles, then pick up the stitches in between. By doing this you won't run out of needles, or knitting, before you reach the required length. Knit one row across all stitches. Set carriage to hold. Begin with the carriage at the side where the point of the V-neck is. Push one needle nearest to the carriage to holding position (automatic wrap) and knit two rows. Repeat this for the depth of the neckband – in 4-ply about 8–12 rows. Hang a claw weight next to the needles in HP, moving it along. It is not necessary to decrease the tension towards the middle as it is for a round neckband because it is lying flat and not following the curve for the neck.

Knit the fold row for the band when the carriage is at the opposite end from the V-shaping. Decrease on the second of the two rows between, and on every alternate row push one needle back to upper working position next to the carriage. When all the needles are in working position, pick up the stitches from the neck edge onto the needles, knit one row across and then cast off round the sinker pins, or take off onto waste yarn to stitch down.

Repeat for the other side of the V. When finished, mattress-stitch the join at the back raglan, or shoulder, and sew up the mitre shape made by the holding position stitches, just catching the edges together. Do not make this a bulky seam.

One word of warning when knitting stripes and a V-neck – try to arrange the stripes so that they do not begin and end exactly at the point of the V. The V-neckband sometimes pulls the knitting up very slightly in the centre. This is not at all obvious on a plain sweater, but if a stripe runs across it, any slight distortion is accentuated. Begin the V-shaping in the centre of a stripe, or begin the stripes above the armhole and V-neck shaping.

When making a patterned garment it is often time-saving to knit both sides of a V-neck together. Obviously this can be done by knitting to the top and using cut-and-sew techniques to shape the neck, but there are two ways of shaping both sides at once, using two cones of yarn.

Method 1
Thread up two identical cones of yarn through the two yarn brakes. Transfer the centre stitch to the next needle for the point of the V. Knit carefully to the centre. When you see the empty needle, take out the first yarn and thread the carriage with the second yarn. Knit back with yarn 2 to centre and replace with yarn 1. Repeat this to the end of the knitting. The stitches decreased to shape the V are moved before knitting the row and as the gap in the centre becomes wider, after two or three rows, it is quite easy to change the yarns in the centre of the knitting.

This is a most useful way of knitting V-necks when knitting lace patterns, because the lace carriage can be taken across all the width of the knitting to transfer stitches, saving half the necessary carriage movements. It can also be used for any other type of pattern, such as tuck and slip. If using it for Fair Isle you will need four yarn brakes to hold duplicate sets of the two colours.

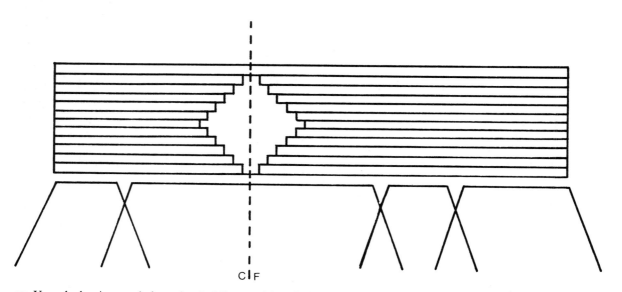

CF

27 V-neck shaping made by using holding position. Left: stitches picked up from top of one raglan and left side of the front neck. Right: stitches picked up from right side of the neck, top of other raglan sleeve, and neck stitches. CF = centre front

Method 2

This method can only be used when knitting stocking-stitch garments, including transfer lace when using a separate lace carriage. The carriage is set for Fair Isle or multicolour knitting and the second cone of yarn is threaded into the second yarn feeder on the sinker plate, as if knitting a colour pattern. Push all needles at the left of the upper working position (push them right forward to holding position, to be sure they will knit correctly) and knit straight across the whole row. The needles in working position will knit with the yarn in feeder A, at the back of the sinker plate, and the needles brought forward will knit with the yarn in feeder B at the front. This must be repeated before knitting every row. Transfer the centre stitches to shape the V before knitting the row.

By knitting both sides together in either of these ways you will ensure that the pattern will match exactly on each side of the V without having to rewind the punchcard and row counter. This is particularly useful when knitting stripes.

28 The V-neckband is shaped by using holding position. The centre line of the V has still to be sewn together

Raglan sleeves

Raglan sleeves produce a popular, easy-fitting style. The armhole is slightly deeper than the set-in sleeve. The length can be adjusted in the rows up to the armhole shaping. The sleeve head is much longer than a set-in sleeve because it includes the length of the shoulder.

The seam of the sleeve to the body must be very neatly made. It cuts right across the front and back of the garment and is very obvious, so it is often best to make a feature of the raglan seam with fully fashioned shaping, or some other pattern. This style is not good for an all-over Fair Isle design because the sloping seams break up the pattern. However, stripes look good with raglan shaping because they continue round the top of the garment in an unbroken line, giving the illusion of a yoke.

When knitted in a 3- or 4-ply yarn, a raglan sleeve usually has one stitch decreased at the beginning of every row, so that it slopes evenly. If a very deep armhole is required, for example for a loose, almost batwing, style of sleeve, then one or two rows must be knitted between the decreasing rows. This can be worked out from the tension square – the number of stitches at the armhole is known, the number required for the neck is known, so the difference between the two is the number to be decreased over the known number of rows needed for the length, half the number for each side.

Decreasing stitches at the edge of the work always tightens the edge. With raglan shaping this must not happen or it will not only be uncomfortable to wear but it will also look puckered when stitched up. Always hang a claw weight on the edge as you knit, moving it up every few rows. This will make the edge stitches larger.

Many patterns can be used to good effect on the raglan seams. Just a few are described here.

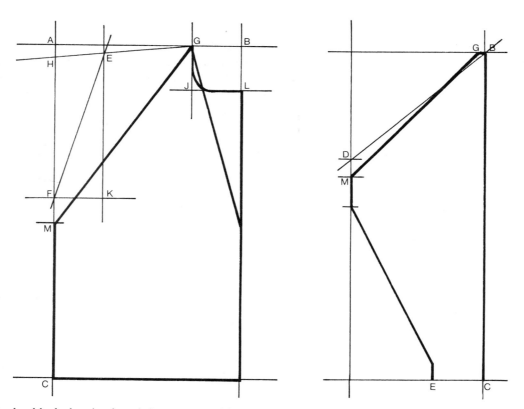

29 Raglan block showing how it is constructed from the basic set-in sleeve design (see fig. 3 for details of measurements)

Body GM = FE + EG   *Sleeve* GM is the same length as on body

A fully fashioned raglan

This always looks very neat, and adds interest to the seam. It is made by decreasing the stitches several needles in from the edge. The multiple transfer tool with the seven adjustable prongs is useful for this as the decreases can be made further from the edge, making a more prominent line. Using the three-pronged transfer tool to move in the third stitch from the edge will leave a line only one stitch wide when the seam is sewn up. (One stitch will be taken by the mattress-stitch seam.) When the knitting becomes too narrow to decrease in this way, continue shaping for the few remaining rows on the edge stitch.

Shell pattern raglan

Although the decreases for this are not made on every row, the number of stitches decreased is still one for every row knitted. Cast off the stitches for the underarm then knit six rows straight. Using the three-pronged transfer tool, take off the three edge stitches and place them onto the next three needles, at both ends of the row. Repeat this until the length required is reached. It may happen that the number of decreases will not quite fit into the rows, so it may be necessary to decrease one or two stitches at the top, instead of three, to get the right number of stitches for the neck. This seam is improved by using the larger transfer tool and so having a line of straight stitches along the edge for sewing up. (See figs 30 and 31.)

Lace raglan

At the beginning of every row, move the two outside stitches in one needle, pick up the next two stitches and move those in one needle, leaving the empty needle in working position. This will make a row of holes all the way up the raglan. For more infrequent holes, decrease on every row by moving the two stitches in one needle, but only move the second pair every four or six rows.

All-in-one raglan

This is a method of making the join for the raglan seam as you knit. The front and the back of the garment are knitted from the bottom upwards in the normal way, but the sleeves are knitted downwards, being joined to the body as they are knitted. This is the neatest method for making a plain raglan seam, and the knitting is quicker.

Knit the back of the garment, but instead of casting off one stitch at the beginning of every row to shape the armhole, put one needle *opposite* the carriage into holding position, set the carriage to hold, knit the row and wrap the yarn round the inside needle in HP. Do this on every row until the armhole is complete. Do not use the automatic wrap – manual wrap makes it easier to insert the transfer tool.

Take off the centre neck stitches onto waste yarn, knit off all the stitches in holding position onto waste yarn, and remove from the machine.

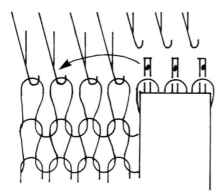

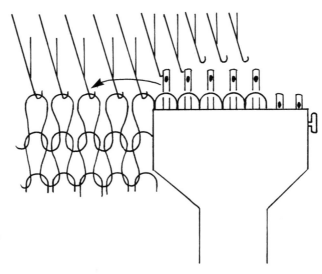

30 Shell edging for decreases on a raglan-sleeved garment *Left* Moving the stitches three needles in from the edge *Right* Decreasing five needles in to leave two stitches knitting straight up the edge

31 The pattern made by decreasing for a shell edging

Knit the front, shaping the neck in the usual way, until only the needles in holding position are left on the machine. Knit off the stitches on the right onto waste yarn and remove from the machine. The other stitches are left in place, and leaving a gap for the top of the sleeve between the two parts, replace the stitches from the back, right-hand side (purl side facing) onto the needles, taking care to pick up the stitch *and* the wrapping yarn onto every needle. Push all the needles to holding position and set carriage to hold.

Make sure that you have replaced the correct stitches onto the machine. The neck edges of back and front should be nearest the centre stitches. Offer up the second piece to the first in the machine as it will be worn, then rotate the back so that the purl side is facing. The stitches uppermost are the ones to be replaced.

Cast on by hand over the empty needles in the

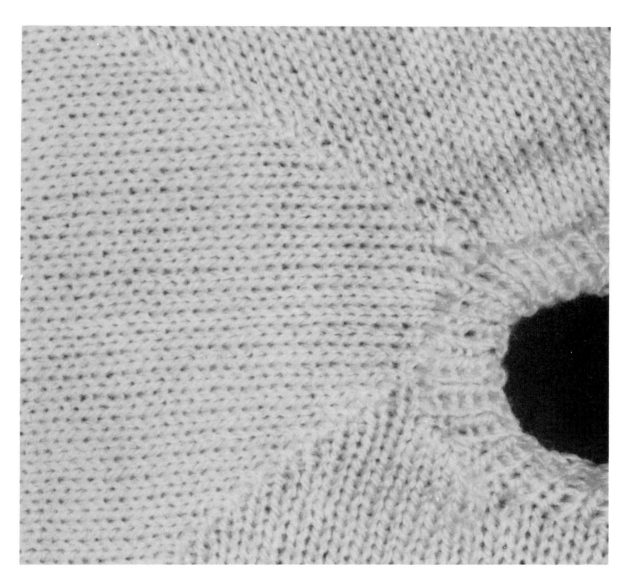

32 The very neat seam made by knitting the raglan sleeve downwards and picking up the stitches from back and front centre. This is the top of the raglan sleeve. Knit two rows by hand, taking the yarn round the end needle in holding position on each row. Hang a claw weight on these stitches.

Knit across the row, always taking the yarn round the inside needle in holding position, nearest to the carriage, and at the same time push one needle opposite the carriage back to upper working position so that it knits on the next row. Continue to do this on every row until all needles are in working position. (There will be three strands of yarn on every needle as you knit it back.)

To make the knitting progress a little quicker, the automatic wrap can be used when replacing the stitches for the sleeves, bringing the needle nearest to the carriage to upper working position. It does look slightly different from the manual wrap, but on the garment in wear it would not be noticed.

Set the row counter to ooo and continue to knit

the sleeve downwards to the cuff, reducing stitches to the number needed at the cuff, evenly.

If you wish to pick up the stitches and knit the neckband onto the garment on the machine, this must be done *before* knitting the second sleeve, in order to knit it in one piece. Pick up the stitches from the front, sleeve top, and back, and then cast on by hand the number of stitches required for the top of the second sleeve. Knit a double band in the usual way.

To knit the second sleeve, replace the raglan stitches from the back onto the machine, pick up the cast-on stitches from the neckband in the centre, and stitches from the front. As there is knitting hanging below the needles for the brushes to grip, there is no need to knit the centre stitches by hand. Leave the raglan stitches (and wrapping threads) in the holding position and knit one row on the centre (sleeve top) stitches. Finish raglan as before, pushing one needle back to upper working position on every row.

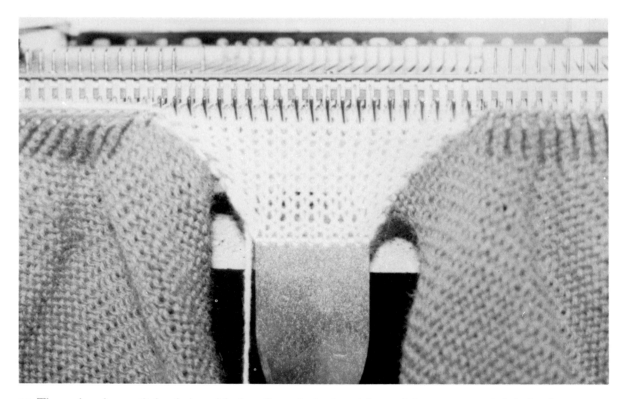

33 The raglan sleeve stitches being picked up from the back and front of the garment as it is knitted. Needles at each side are in holding position, one brought back to knit on every row. Sleeve section knitted in a contrast colour

ADVANTAGES

1 This method gives a very neat raglan seam.

2 There is less sewing up to do.

3 The raglan seam is never tight.

4 Knitting the sleeve downwards means that the length can easily be adjusted, e.g. for children's garments, or a damaged cuff can easily be replaced.

DISADVANTAGES

1 This method can only be done on a raglan shaping where the stitches are reduced on every row.

2 If you are using a pattern, you must remember to turn over the card, or reverse the pattern on the electronic sheet, for the sleeves, to knit it upside down.

3 It is not always possible to knit the neckband on.

4 Using a hem at the cuff presents no problems, but with a true rib cuff the cast-off edge is not as neat as the cast-on for the rib.

Raglan sweater with all-in-one sleeve

To fit 71 76 81 86 91 96 101 107 cm
      28 30 32 34 36 38 40 42 in.

Materials 4-ply acrylic 280–400gm or use 3 strands 2/30 knitted together

Add your own pattern and adjust tension accordingly or knit plain as pattern tension.

Tension 28 sts and 40 rows to 10cm (4 in.) at MT approx 7

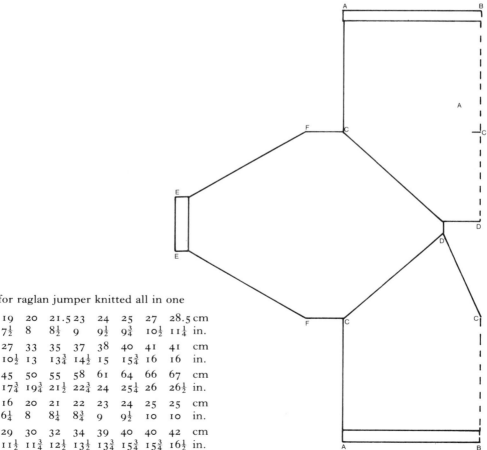

34 Diagram for raglan jumper knitted all in one

AB = 19   20   21.5 23   24   25   27   28.5 cm
     7½   8   8½   9   9½   9¾   10½   11¼ in.

BC = 27   33   35   37   38   40   41   41   cm
     10½   13   13¾   14½   15   15¾   16   16   in.

BD = 45   50   55   58   61   64   66   67   cm
     17¾   19¾   21½   22¾   24   25¼   26   26½ in.

EE = 16   20   21   22   23   24   25   25   cm
     6¼   8   8¼   8¾   9   9½   10   10   in.

FF = 29   30   32   34   39   40   40   42   cm
     11½   11¾   12½   13½   13¾   15¾   15¾   16½ in.

PATTERN NOTES

1 Sometimes people get so carried away with the idea of putting needles to holding position for the neck and sleeves that they try to do the same with the V-neck shaping. This is *not* possible when knitting vertically because you are not casting off the stitches on every row. The needles in holding position would have several rows of knitting between them.

2 The following pattern can, of course, be knitted with a round neck. Use the block from the basic pattern (chapter 2).

3 To knit a raglan-sleeved jumper without the all-in-one sleeve, follow these instructions but cast off the armhole stitches to give the design you want. Reverse sleeve instructions and knit from cuff to neck in the usual way.

BACK

Using WY cast on 100 108 121 127 135 141 147 155 sts.
Knit a few rows.
Change to MY or sewing thread and MT − 2.
Knit 2 rows with sewing thread.
Knit 18 rows with MY, then 1 loose fold row.
Knit 20 rows at MT − 2.
Fill the needles and then pick up stitches in sewing thread and place on needles.
RC 000.
Knit 90 110 120 128 134 140 142 142 rows.

Shape armhole
On next 2 rows, push 1 1 2 2 2 2 3 3 sts to HP at opposite end to carr. Hang claw weights. On every row push needle at end opposite carr to HP, always wrapping inside needle.
RC 162 188 202 212 226 236 244 248 rows leaving 38 38 39 41 43 45 45 45 sts for back neck. Take these off onto WY or garter bar. Push needles back. Release all HP sts from machine on several rows of WY.

FRONT

Knit as back to 92 112 122 130 134 142 144 144 rows.

Shape V-neck
Divide work into two halves by pushing all needles at side opposite to carr to HP. Knit on right side only. Hang claw weights at each side, moving them in as you knit. Still continuing to decrease at armhole edge as for back, cast off 1 st at neck edge at beg of 4th row and every following 4th row until only 1 remains. Cast off.
RC 162 188 202 212 226 236 244 248.
Take off all armhole sts onto a few rows WY.
Complete left-hand side to match, reversing the shapings. Do not remove sts in HP from the machine.

FIRST SLEEVE

Leave a gap of 10 10 10 12 12 14 14 14 needles at neck end of front, for top of sleeve.
Replace sts from left-hand-side raglan of back onto needles next to space, neck edge to centre, wrong side facing. Two threads on every needle. Push all needles to HP, set carr to hold.
Cast on (e-wrap) over empty centre needles, and knit 2 rows by hand. Hang a claw weight on these stitches.
Return 1 needle to UWP at beg of every row, until all needles are in WP.
RC 000.
Knit 18 20 30 32 34 30 20 15 rows.
Dec 1 st at beg of next 2 rows and every 6th 7th, 7th 8th, 7th 8th, 7th 8th, 6th 7th, 5th 6th, 5th 6th, 5th 6th rows (50 56 58 60 64 66 68 68 sts).
Knit to RC 115 134 156 158 160 160 160 160.
Transfer every 3rd st for mock rib MT − 3.
Knit 20 rows. Knit 1 loose row for fold. MT − 4, knit 20 rows. Take off on WY and stitch up hem. Before knitting the second sleeve knit the neck-band.

NECKBAND

With wrong side facing, replace sts from back neck and top of first sleeve (approx 52 60 89 94 99 103 104 106 sts) from left front neck (total of 98 104 129 135 141 147 149 153 sts).
Knit 1 row at MT. Transfer every 3rd st for mock rib MT−2 (approx 5), pushing 1 needle to HP at point of V on every row. Knit 8 rows.
Knit 1 loose fold row. Knit 8 rows at MT − 2 bringing 1 needle on every row to UWP so that it knits.
Remove on WY and stitch down, or pick up first row of neckband.
Knit 1 row at MT. Cast off loosely.

Right side of neck

Pick up the same number of sts from the other front neck, and cast on 10 10 10 12 14 14 14 14 sts to the right of it for top of second sleeve. Knit 1 row.

Complete to match other side, shaping mitre at point of V.

SECOND SLEEVE

Pick up top of sleeve sts in centre from neckband and leave in WP.

Replace raglan sleeve sts from back and front in HP. Knit as first sleeve.

TO MAKE UP

Sew all seams and complete welts as necessary.

Children's raglan jumpers

The basic method of knitting an all-in-one raglan in smaller sizes is the same as for the adult garment. The basic block will give a guide to the numbers of stitches and rows required. The only difference is that an opening is needed on a round neck to make the neck larger. This is made when knitting the second sleeve. Do not replace the top 10 or 12 stitches onto the needles from the back raglan. The needles are pushed to holding position and returned to working position one at a time in the same way as the others. The sleeve edge at the top is then left open and a narrow band can be picked up onto the stitches from the back and the side of the sleeve to make a buttoned opening.

Variations on the all-in-one raglan

Before knitting the sleeve it is possible to introduce some patterns along the line of the raglan.

It is not practicable to make these sections of pattern too wide, because they will make the neck larger too. If you think the neck will be a little tight as you have knitted it then this is one way of enlarging it. The type of pattern to be knitted should be considered carefully. You are knitting rows sideways onto stitches and the proportion of the stitch means that the knitting will be tighter knitted across these stitches, so increase the tension.

1 *Stripes* Just two rows of another colour will accentuate the seam. Increase the tension for these rows by one number to ensure that they do not pull the knitting in.

2 *A small Fair Isle pattern* (not more than four or five rows wide) Increase the tension by at least two whole numbers for these rows.

3 *Rows of holes for a lacy look* Do not wrap the needles in holding position when knitting.

4 *Winding pattern* Do this on the empty needles before replacing the stitches. This means that all the stitches need to be removed, even the last set from the front as given in the pattern, so that the needles can be wrapped. Using contrast yarn, e-wrap all the needles which will have the raglan stitches replaced onto them. Put the stitches on back top. Try winding the yarn twice round some needles, or over two needles together, to give a more solid effect.

Sideways-knitted all-in-one raglan

The second method of knitting a raglan jumper all in one piece is to knit it sideways. All the shaping is done by holding position as before. The sleeve seams are the only ones which have to be joined. The knitting needs to be started in an area of plain knitting, without any shaping, usually the centre back. Start and begin with waste yarn and graft this seam very carefully. This is one place where grafting is really necessary to make a good join.

If this pattern is to be made into a cardigan, it is easiest to start at the centre front so that you begin and end with the bands. Knitting sideways allows vertical patterns to be made: stripes, Fair Isle, bands of thicker yarn woven in. If you introduce patterns, ensure that they will be symmetrical on the garment. This means that you must work out exactly the number of rows from your tension square, and exactly where you want the stripes to come. Stripes which fall just off centre on the front will look wrong if they are all evenly spaced out. A design that is deliberately asymmetrical must be obviously so.

To shape the raglan seams the needles are pushed into holding position one at a time and then returned to upper working position one at a time in the reverse order. The inside needle in holding position must be wrapped every time, but the automatic wrap can be used on every row as no stitches are to be picked up again.

In the pattern that follows the side of the sleeve is not shaped at all. It looks attractive as a full sleeve gathered into the cuff. If you wish to have a tapered sleeve then the sides must be cast on with an e-wrap in blocks of stitches. The final length must be reached before the armhole shaping is finished so that the full width of the cuff can be knitted.

All-in-one sideways-knitted jumper

To fit	81	to	91	100	to	116	cm
	32	to	36	38	to	42	in.

Length   56cm (22 in.)   60cm (23½ in.)

Sleeve length 33.5cm (13 in.)   35cm (13¾ in.)

Materials   Total of 250gm: approx 80gm 2/30 Atkinsons Superbright, approx 170gm Atkinsons Poodle. Two ends of Superbright used for garment, one of Poodle. For welts and collar three ends of Superbright.

Tension   29 sts and 56 rows to 10cm (4 in.) at MT approx 4

PATTERN NOTES

1 The knit side is used as the right side.

2 The hem is knitted onto the bottom of the jumper. Because it can't be knitted at a tighter tension than the rest of the garment it will hang straight. A cord threaded through the hem turns it into a blouson style.

3 If you wish to make a tighter hem, rather than gathering up with a cord, use one of the following methods:

(a) The left 30 stitches can be left off the knitting altogether, and after the garment is finished stitches can be picked up from along the bottom edge and a hem knitted on at a tighter tension.

(b) Put the left 30 stitches into holding position at intervals so that fewer rows are knitted on them. For example, by pushing the 30 stitches to holding position every 20 rows for one row, the width around the bottom will be reduced by about 10 cm (4 in.).

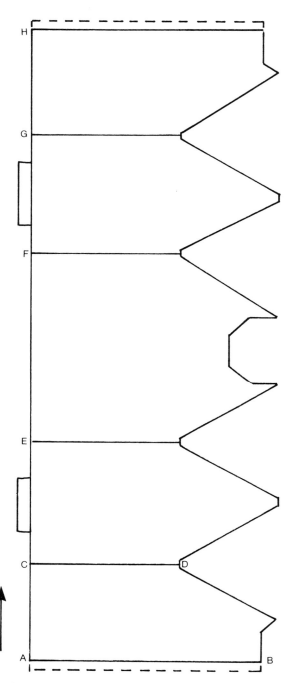

35 Diagram for sideways-knitted all-in one jumper

AB =	56	60	cm	EF =	44	46	cm
	22	23½	in.		17¼	18	in.
CD =	33.5	35	cm	FG =	33	35	cm
	13¼	13¾	in.		13	13¾	in.
AC =	22	23	cm	GH =	22	23	cm
	8½	9	in.		8½	9	in.
CE =	33	35	cm				
	13	13¾	in.				

4 The needle left out of work on the back and front of the garment is not required on the sleeve, where the cuff will be picked up and knitted on afterwards. Bring the needle to working position in the middle of the rows knitted in waste yarn between back and sleeve/front and sleeve. Transfer it back to the next needle, and leave the needle in non-working position, during the next waste yarn knitting.

5 Sleeve seam measures 32–34cm (12½–13½ in.) plus the welt of about 3cm (1¼ in.) knitted on afterwards. If a longer sleeve is needed then more stitches have to be cast on at the left of the needle bed. Do this in the middle of the waste yarn section. When the sleeve is finished, knit a few rows in the waste yarn then release the extra stitches from the machine, push the needles back to non-working position and continue with the next body section.

6 A full sleeve should not be made too long or the fullness will hang over the cuff. The raglan shaping of this design comes quite low down, and a slightly longer welt may be all that is needed if the sleeve seems short.

7 *Grafting the seams* The underarm sleeve seam can be grafted. There will be three rows of Superbright instead of two here, one from each end of knitting and the one made by the grafting stitch. This will not show in this position. However, on the back of the garment it must give the correct sequence of rows. There will be one row of Superbright and one row of Poodle to graft together. Care must be taken that the stitch of Poodle yarn is correctly picked up.

Start at centre back
Cast on with WY   153 sts, 85 to left of 0 and 73 to right
165 sts, 85 to left of 0 and 80 to right.

Knit a few rows. Transfer 12th st from the left to next needle and leave needle in NWP. Change to MY and MT.
Beg with Superbright, knit 1 row, then continue in pattern sequence of 10 rows Poodle, 2 rows Superbright throughout.
Knit to RC 35 40.
Inc 1 st right on every row to needle number 80 85 at right.
RC 40 45.

* At right bring 1 needle to HP on every row to RC 117 122.
Knit straight for 6 rows ending with 1 row Superbright.
Cancel row tripper, but not counter.
Knit a few rows in WY. Knit 1 row with nylon cord. Knit a few rows WY ** bringing to WP the needle in NWP at left for fold of hem.

SLEEVE
*** Engage row tripper.
Change to MY. Beg with 1 row Superbright, knit 6 rows, then 1 needle to UWP at right on every row until all needles are in WP ****.
RC 209 214.
Knit 24 rows straight.
Knit from * to **. Transfer 12th needle from right to next needle for fold of hem.
Pick up sts from last row of back, before WY, onto needles.
Knit from *** to ****.
RC 399 404.

Shape front neck
Cast off 15 sts at beg of next row at right, then 1 st at beg of every row to 120 130 sts.
Knit straight for 25 rows.
RC 440 445.
Increase 1 st at right on next 25 rows. Cast on 15 sts at right (160 170 sts).
RC 494 499.
Repeat from * to ****.
RC 660 665.
Knit 24 rows straight.
Repeat from * to ***.
Pick up sts from second side of front onto needles and continue to knit second half of back.
Decrease 1 st at right for next 5 rows.
Knit 35 40 rows straight. Take off onto WY, last row being knitted in Poodle.

CUFFS
Cast on 60 sts with WY. Knit a few rows, change to MY and MT + 1.
Using 3 ends of Superbright knit 30 rows, gradually dec tension to MT − 1 (approx 3). Knit 1 loose row.
Knit 30 rows, gradually inc tension to MT + 1.
Pick up sts from first row in MY onto needles.
Knit 1 row.

Pick up cuff end of sleeve onto needles with wrong side facing, gathering sleeve into cuff. Knit 1 row and cast off loosely.

Alternatively you can take off onto WY and stitch the cuff onto the end of the sleeve on both sides.

COLLAR

At extreme left side of needle bed cast on 60 sts in WY.

Change to 3 ends Superbright and knit 2 rows at MT + 2 (approx 6).

Use the pattern sequence of 6 rows Superbright and 2 rows Poodle throughout the collar.

At beginning of *every* row, left dec 1 st, and at right inc 1 st.

Continue to knit like this, gradually moving across the needle bed. The full length of the needle bed should be enough. When the last needle at the right is brought out to be knitted, the collar should be long enough.

Knit 2 rows and take off onto WY.

If the collar is still not long enough to fit the neck, replace sts onto the left side of bed and continue to knit.

Graft back seam of jumper

Graft the first and last rows of the collar together and sew onto the neck of the jumper. The collar should be allowed to roll over the neck to form a cowl.

36 The pattern made by thick and thin yarns on raglan shaping and the diagonally knitted cowl collar

TO MAKE UP

Graft together the sleeve seams.

Turn up the bottom edge of the body of the garment to make a hem, using the line of the non-working position needle as a guide for the bottom edge.

Using three ends of Superbright over five stitches, make a cord and thread it through the hem. This will pouch up the bottom of the jumper to give a blouson effect.

To knit a V-neck on a sideways-knitted garment

The neck can be shaped by using holding position. Knit the first shoulder then push groups of needles at neck end to holding position on alternate rows, about four or five at a time, until the depth of the V is reached and you have knitted halfway across the front. Knit all the stitches on the needles in holding position onto waste yarn. Knit one row with nylon cord and a few more rows of waste. Do not remove from the machine. Push all the neck needles back to holding position and while knitting the other half of the neck return them a few at a time to working position until all are knitted. Knit the second shoulder. Pull out the nylon cord and the two halves of the V will part. The stitches held on the waste yarn are to be picked up for the neckband.

Knitting a yoked jumper

The shape for this is based on the raglan shape, so you can use any raglan pattern as a basis for the number of stitches and rows required, the only difference being that the top of the sleeve and the body are knitted together and the slope of the raglan is made at the shoulder edge. The yoke usually begins just above the armhole shaping.

Always knit the sleeves first up to the yoke. Mark the centre stitch and take off the stitches at the top onto two separate lengths of waste yarn.

Knit the back of the body of the jumper up to the armhole shaping and then replace half the stitches from each sleeve on needles at each side of the back. Set row counter to 000. Knit the first Fair Isle pattern, increasing the tension, and when the first plain row after the pattern has been knitted decrease across the row by transferring two stitches for every row knitted to the next needle. For example, for 12 rows knitted transfer 12 stitches spaced evenly to left of 0 and 12 stitches to the right reducing number of stitches by 24. Push the empty needle back to working position. If you have a separate lace carriage the transfers can be done quickly with this. Knit several rows over the remaining stitches with waste yarn and strip off. Bring empty needles back to working position and push 12 needles at each end back to non-working position and replace the stitches onto remaining needles. If all the decreases are made on the plain rows the Fair Isle pattern does not get distorted. Also you are only dealing with one yarn instead of two.

The neck shaping is below the yoke. The yoke pattern is knitted in straight lines of Fair Isle, so in order to lower the neck at the front, the body of the jumper is shaped by placing needles into holding position at each side to make a curve. A shallower curve is made on the back. This curved shape is echoed at the neckline.

Using a garter bar

A garter bar consists of two or three lengths of metal with prongs like the transfer tool along one edge which can be used to remove long lengths of stitches from the needles. It can be used to hold stitches ready to return them quickly to the machine, or the work can be turned over and the

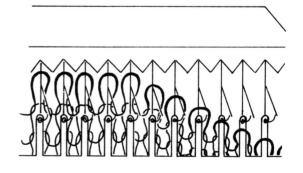

37 Using the garter bar. The stitches at the right are being pulled off the needles onto the prongs of the garter bar. The stopper strip is at the back of the bed behind the stitches

stitches returned to the needles facing the other way. If this is repeated twice on the yoke row, purl stitches would be knitted between the Fair Isle patterns. Practise this technique first before trying it on a garment. A long section of rows of garter stitch would be very tedious to do on the machine.

Garter stitch

Use the length of garter bar needed. Two lengths may need to be clipped together if there are more than 100 stitches. Pull all needles forward to holding position and ensure that all latches are open. Place the stopper strip behind the needles so that the serrated edge comes over the sinker pins and teeth fit between the needles and behind the stitches on the needles. This keeps the needles in the forward position so that you will not inadvertently push them back with the bar. Also, if you have any needles which are slightly bent they will be held straight so that it is easier to slide the stitches off. Place the holes of the garter bar over the hooks with the grooved side *upwards*. Begin at one end and continue across the row, pulling the stitches firmly forward on the needles. If you pull forward in several places some stitches may catch on the hooks and you will have to start again. As the latches close, the stitches will slip onto the prongs of the bar. Pull them right down to the bottom of the prongs where they will be held securely. Unhook the bar from the needles and turn the work round so that the knit side of the fabric is facing. Make sure all the latches are open on the needles. Lay the garter bar on top of the needles still in holding position, with the grooves on the needle hooks. You can see the tips of the latches through the bar holes. As you pull the garter bar towards you the stitches will catch on the hooks of the needles and the garter bar will slide off. It always looks as though the knitted fabric will end up on top of the needles, but as the garter bar is removed the knitting will fall into place below the needles. Taking care not to catch the holes of the garter bar on the needle hooks, pull the bar downwards and push it slightly away from you to remove it from the stitches. Knit one row and repeat the process.

Decreasing within the row

To take stitches off the needles and return them, closing up the gaps to make the decreases, it is easier to do this in two halves.

Bring all needles to holding position, including empty ones where transfers were made. Place one section of stopper bar in position, as before, behind the stitches on the right half of the needles. Place a second section of stopper strip *in front of* the stitches on the left half of the needles. This is going to stop the stitches at this side from pulling off the needles as those on the right are removed. Two or three stitches near the centre will pull forward. Hang a three-pronged transfer tool on these. Take the stitches off onto the right-hand bar, push extra needles back. Replace the stitches onto the needles from the right-hand bar a few at a time. As an empty prong is reached where the stitch has been decreased, take the bar off and re-hook so that the next stitch will slip back onto the empty needle. Repeat for the other half of the stitches.

If the garter bar is used to hold stitches for replacement onto the needles later, perhaps for a neckband, then the prongs can be covered with plastic binding strip (such as is used for hanging posters), and held in place with elastic bands so that the stitches do not pull off.

Pattern for a yoked jumper

To fit	81	86	91	97	101	cm
	32	34	36	38	40	in

Materials   Main colour 280–320gm Shetland wool from Simply Shetland. Small amounts (about 30gm) of 4 colours

Tension   29 sts and 41 rows to 10cm (4 in.) measured over washed tension swatch, at MT approx 8.2

PATTERN NOTES

1 The punchcard shown in fig. 39 is for some traditional Fair Isle patterns. The wider ones are interspersed with narrow bands which are called 'peerie' patterns. The designs can be knitted all in the same colour, a different colour can be used for each complete pattern, or each pattern can be knitted in two colours. For example, you could use three shades of pink, so that the colours were graduated from dark to light from the outside to

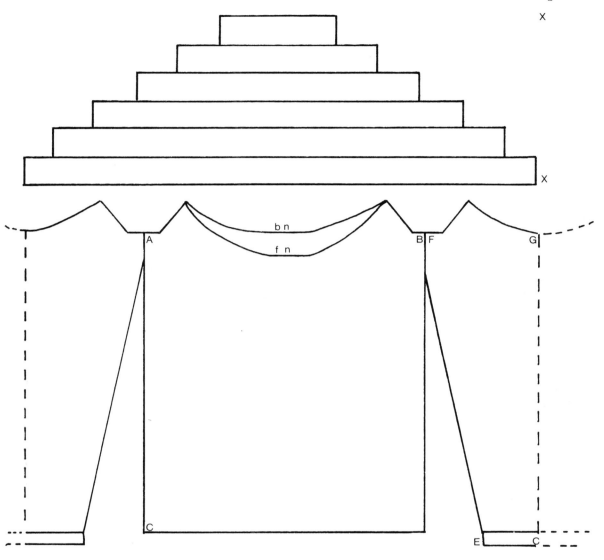

38 Diagram for yoked jumper pattern

Body	AB =	44	47	49	51	53	cm
		$17\frac{1}{4}$	$18\frac{1}{2}$	$19\frac{1}{4}$	20	21	in.
	AC =	36	36	39	39	41	cm
		$14\frac{1}{4}$	$14\frac{1}{4}$	$15\frac{1}{4}$	$15\frac{1}{4}$	16	in.

fn = front neck

bn = back neck

Sleeve	EC =	10.5	11	11.5	12	13	cm
		4	$4\frac{1}{4}$	$4\frac{1}{2}$	$4\frac{3}{4}$	5	in.
	GC =	44	44	45	46	47	cm
		$17\frac{1}{4}$	$17\frac{1}{4}$	$17\frac{3}{4}$	18	$18\frac{1}{2}$	in.
	FG =	19.5	20	20	20.5	22	cm
		$7\frac{3}{4}$	8	8	8	$8\frac{3}{4}$	in.

Depth of yoke	15	16	16	17	17	cm
	6	$6\frac{1}{4}$	$6\frac{1}{4}$	$6\frac{3}{4}$	$6\frac{3}{4}$	in.

the centre of the design. In order to do this there must be an even number of rows to each pattern – otherwise the yarns will end up on opposite sides of the knitting. At least two rows can then be knitted in each colour. The peerie patterns are knitted in a fourth colour to separate the main patterns.

2 The punchcard can be used for all sizes. End the Fair Isle yoke with a complete pattern or rows of plain knitting. Do not end at the neck in the middle of a pattern. If you can't fit in a larger pattern, knit one of the peerie patterns again or knit more rows of stocking stitch.

3 The punchcard for the handspun waistcoat in chapter 11 is also made up of traditional Fair Isle designs. These can be substituted to make a more masculine garment if desired, rather than using the bow and hearts.

4 The neckband can be knitted all in one piece for back and front in the usual way but it is simpler, since all the neck stitches are on the machine and there are none to pick up each side, to knit it directly onto the garment as you finish the yoke, in two pieces. Mattress-stitch the two halves carefully together.

5 The cast-off stitch at the end of the armhole shapings, before beginning the yoke, is used in sewing up the seam.

6 The cast-on stitch at each shoulder edge is used in sewing up the seam.

SLEEVES
Knit these first.
Bring forward 62 66 68 70 72 needles.
Push every 3rd needle to NWP and cast on with WY over remainder, for mock rib.
Knit a few rows. Change to MT − 3 and MY.
Knit 20 rows. Knit 1 row at MT + 2.
Return to MT − 2 and knit 20 rows.
Bring all needles to WP and pick up sts for hem, filling empty needles with a stitch.
RC 00.
Change to MT, inc at beg of next 2 rows and every 5th and 6th rows following to 110 114 114 120 122 sts.
RC 148 150 154 158 168 rows.

Shape armhole
Cast off 4 sts at beg of next 2 rows.

Cast off 1 st at beg of next 2 rows.
At side nearest carr leave 30 30 33 34 36 sts in WP and push all others to HP. Set carr to hold.
Still dec at armhole edge, at beg of alt rows push 1 needle to HP at inside edge on every row to 1 st. Cast off.
Repeat for the other side.
Take sts off onto WY in two halves.

BACK
Bring forward 124 148 158 160 168 needles.
Cast on and make hem as on sleeves.
RC 000.
Change to MT and knit to RC 144 132 140 146 154.

Shape armhole
Cast off 4 sts at beg of next 2 rows.
Cast off 1 st at beg of next 2 rows.
At side nearest to the carr leave 26 28 28 30 30 needles in WP. Push all others to HP and set carr to hold.
Still dec at armhole edge at beg of alt rows, push 1 needle to HP at neck edge on every row. Cast off last st.
Repeat for the other side.

YOKE
Replace half sts from each sleeve onto needles at each side of back, centre of each sleeve to outside edge. Cast on 1 st each end (total of 190 196 196 198 200 sts).
RC 000.
Knit 1 row over all sts.
Engage punchcard and lock on first row. Knit 1 row to select needle for first pattern.
Change to MT + 1 for Fair Isle. Using contrast colours knit 2 rows with colour A, 1 row with colour B. Do not break yarn but leave at side of machine. 2 rows colour C, 1 row colour B, 2 rows colour A.
Knit 2 rows main colour only.
RC 12.
Select 12 needles evenly spaced each side of 0 and transfer to next needle.
Push empty needles to NWP, knit 1 row.
Take off on WY (or garter bar).
Push back 12 needles each end to NWP. Return NWP needles to WP.
Replace sts on needles (178 184 184 186 188 sts).

Knit 1 row, and knit next pattern using colour D. Knit 2 rows.

RC 20, 8 rows knitted since last transfer. Repeat transfer process after each pattern, moving 2 sts for every row knitted to 74 80 80 82 84 sts.
Knit 8 more rows.
RC 60 68 68 70 72.

NECKBAND

Transfer every 3rd st to next needle for mock rib neckband. Change to MT − 1.
Knit 20 rows, gradually dec to MT − 4. Knit 1 loose row for fold.
Knit 20 rows, gradually inc from MT − 4 to MT − 1.
Take off on WY and sew down inside through every st.

FRONT

Cast on and knit as back to RC 134 136 146 148 156.
At side nearest to carr leave 38 40 40 42 42 needles in WP. Push all others to NWP.
On next 12 rows push one needle at neck edge to HP on every row.

Shape armhole
Next row cast off 4 sts at side opposite to neck. 1 needle to HP at neck.
Continue to knit, shaping armhole by casting off 1 st at beg of alt rows, while pushing 1 needle to HP at neck edge on every row. Cast off last st.
Repeat at other side.

FRONT YOKE

Replace other half of sleeve sts onto needles each side of front.
Centre of sleeve to outside, cast on 1 st each end.
Knit yoke and neckband as for back.

TO MAKE UP

Carefully mattress-stitch the shoulder seams, taking in only the extra stitch cast on at each side. Mattress-stitch the underarm seams, taking in the extra stitch which was cast off at yoke. Sew up side and sleeve seams. The garment should be washed before wear.

39 Traditional Fair Isle designs for the yoke of the jumper. The wider patterns are interspersed with the narrow 'peerie' patterns

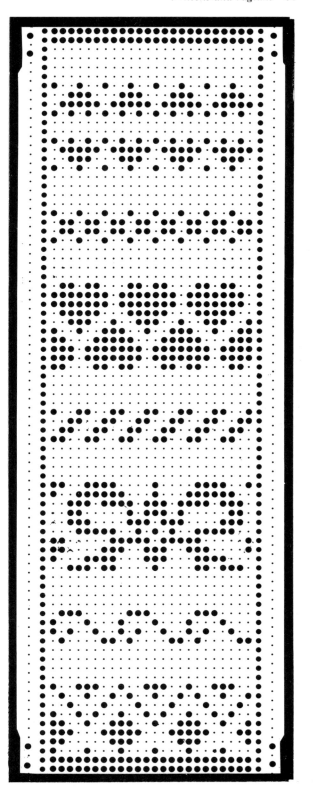

CHAPTER 5

Skirts

Many people feel they cannot wear a knitted skirt because they are not an elegant, tall size 12, but in fact they are suitable for everyone provided they are made large enough. Skirts which 'cling' are not attractive so be honest about your hip measurement. Add at least 5 cm (2 in.) for ease and that is the size you must knit.

Select the yarn carefully for a skirt. Remember that you will be pressing it with warmth every time you sit down. Some acrylic fabrics crease easily or may 'seat'. Textured yarns such as bouclés have more spring to them and, as with wool, wool mixtures and cottons, will resist creasing and recover their shape better. However, so long as you are aware of the limitations of some fabrics, a wide variety can be used, and since knitted skirts do not usually have a definite back or front, then the skirt can be turned round every time it is worn to a different position and it will not pull out of shape.

While the normal tension swatch will indicate the numbers of stitches and rows required, when the skirt is being worn the weight of the material may make the skirt drop and lengthen, so knit a much larger piece – the full length of the skirt, and leave it to hang overnight before measuring.

Because the weight on the stitches is different on a sideways-knitted garment it may drop more than one that is knitted from the bottom. After measuring even quite a large tension swatch it is advisable to subtract two stitches per 10cm (4 in.) of length. This allows for the altered hang of the fabric.

When using acrylics to knit a skirt, a nice shape can be obtained by damp pressing after finishing. Although this flattens the fabric, it allows it to fall softly and gives it a swing – the exception that proves the rule! Practise first on the tension swatch.

Instructions for various waistbands and hem finishes for skirts follow the patterns in this chapter. These can be substituted for those given in the patterns if you wish, or if they are more suitable for the yarn you use.

Sideways-knitted skirts

These are very quick to make. There is only one seam to join up and if the yarn used is not too thick then a separate waistband need not be knitted. The top edge of the skirt can be turned over and elastic threaded through. The bottom edge may require some finishing, but some yarns will lay flat when pressed, especially when using shadow pleating as in the first pattern.

Shadow-pleated skirt

Size	Length 69 cm (27 in.)
To fit hips	86 to 91cm 96 to 101cm 106 to 111cm 34 to 36 in. 38 to 40 in. 42 to 44 in.
Materials	One cone Atkinson's Poodle yarn, one cone of Atkinson's Superbright 2/30. One strand from both cones used for the thicker stripes, and one strand of Superbright used for the thinner stripes
Tension	31 sts and 64 rows to 10cm (4 in.) at MT 3.2

PATTERN NOTES

1 Two thicknesses of yarn are required. The thicker yarn should be a 3- or 4-ply equivalent (2/10 or 2/8). This can either be Shetland wool, three strands of 2/30, or a bouclé 2-ply (2/16) plus one strand of 2/20.

2 The finer yarn can be one strand of 2/30 or a fine 2-ply. If it is any thicker than this the 'pleats' will not be distinct.

3 The skirt is a straight piece, with no shaping.

4 Thread each yarn through a separate tension wire on the yarn mast. The Poodle yarn can then be removed easily and held with one hand away from the machine while knitting with the thinner one only.

5 If you are using two smooth yarns, not a bouclé, then it does not matter whether you begin with the thin or the thick yarn, but by starting with a smooth yarn it will be easier to see, and to pick up, the stitches to join up the skirt when it is finished.

Cast on 200 sts using WY. Knit a few rows.
Knit 1 row with nylon cord.
Knit 2 rows with 2/30.
Join in the Poodle yarn, and using both yarns together knit 6 rows.
Repeat these 8 rows, keeping the same tension throughout for 576 640 704 rows.
End with 6 rows of thick yarn. Do not remove from the machine.
Since the purl side of the skirt will be the right side (this is where the pleated effect is seen), the first row of stitches above the nylon cord can be picked up onto the same needles (knit sides together). One needle at a time, pull the second stitch through the first, so that there is only one stitch left on each needle. Knit one row at a loose tension and cast off behind the sinker pins, or with a latch tool. Do not pull the work tight.

TO MAKE UP

When the knitting is removed from the machine, pull it sideways to close up the pleats. A small hem may be turned over at the top and elastic threaded through or other waistband added.

Lightly press the skirt so that the bottom edge flares out slightly below the hips. This will stop it clinging and make it fall straight. No hem or other finish should be needed at the bottom of the skirt.

Variations for shadow pleats

These can be made by using different numbers of rows of each thickness of yarn. For example, 2 rows thick, 2 rows thin, 4 rows thin, repeated.

Do not knit too wide a strip in the thinner yarn or the skirt will be flimsy and 'see-through' and it may pull out of shape because the tension is rather loose for the thickness of the yarn. Wider strips of the thicker yarn can be used without it having this effect. These varied stripes may make a little difference to the number of rows to be knitted to balance the pattern, but the difference should only be a matter of a few rows and since the tension is the same throughout and the 'pleats' have a stretchy effect it will make an insignificant difference to the overall size.

Variations in colour can also be used on the mock pleats. One yarn can be darker than the other, or three or more colours can be used to give a panelled effect. However, if, say, you are going to knit one set of six rows in another colour every six sections, you may have to knit extra rows on the last section in order to make the sequence even. Unless you have already planned a very loose fit, it is better to knit a few extra rows rather than less. (See fig. 10).

Circular skirts

The circular skirt is the type of sideways-knitted skirt that is perhaps the easiest to wear. The skirt is shaped by putting needles into holding position at the end of the needle bed where the waist is to be, so that more rows are knitted round the hem than at the top. This style gives opportunities for many variations in pattern and colour in vertical stripes, which are flattering to most figures. A section of straight rows is knitted between the shaped pieces and it is on these that the patterns – lace, Fair Isle, etc. – may be included.

True pleats can be made on this style of skirt either by altering the tension of the stitches or by using tuck and slip stitches. The pattern given here uses the second method.

1 *Altering the tensions* If a loose row is knitted the fabric will fold towards the purl side, as has been shown when knitting a hem. A tight row of stitches will make it fold in the opposite direction towards the knit side, so by alternating loose and tight rows of stitches with an even gap between them the material will concertina into pleats. The pleats will need to be pressed to make them sharp, but will hold quite well.

2 *Using tuck and slip stitches*   Tuck stitches act upon the knitting in the same way as the loose rows. They tend to fold the fabric towards the purl side. Slip stitches react in the opposite direction when isolated amongst stocking stitch knitting. These pleats are even more permanent.

Pleated circular skirt

Size	Finished length 69cm (27 in.)
To fit hips	86 96 106 cm
	34 38 42 in.
Materials	4-ply Shetland wool from Jamieson and Smith.
Tension	28 sts and 40 rows to 10cm (4 in.) at MT approx 8

40 Several types of mock pleat, made by varying the rows knitted in the thick and thin yarns

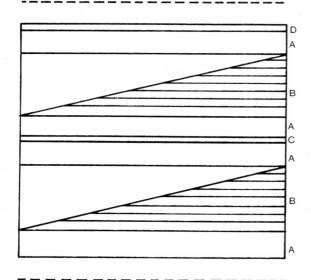

41 Begin and end skirt with waste yarn. This complete section is repeated for full width required to make a pleated skirt

A straight section of knitting
B shaped section with needles in holding position
C two rows of tuck stitch
D two rows of slip stitch

Insert card 1 (alternate needles selected), locked throughout on row 1.
Using WY cast on 200 sts. Knit a few rows, then knit 1 row with nylon cord. This may seem too many stitches according to the tension, but allowance has been made for a 4-cm (1½-in.) turnover at the top for a casing for elastic.
Change to MT and Shetland wool.
Knit 4 6 8 rows. COR.
* At left side of needle bed bring 9 needles to HP. Set carr to hold. Knit 1 row.
Bring 1 needle to HP at left of needle bed (next to carr) and knit the row (automatic wrap).
Repeat this until there are only 10 needles left in WP, at right of bed. Set carr to knit all needles back on next row.
Knit 5 7 9 rows.
Set carr to select pattern needles and knit 1 row.**
Set carr to tuck. Knit 2 rows.
Cancel tuck setting, and reset machine for st st.
Knit 6 8 10 rows.
Knit from * to ** once more.
Set carr to slip, knit 2 rows.

Cancel slip setting and reset the carr to knit st st. Knit 6 8 10 rows.***
Repeat from * to *** 8 times (total of 9 times, making 18 pleats).
Be careful that you make each fold of tuck and slip alternately.
After the last 2 rows of the 18th pleat (slip rows), knit only *one* row and take off with several rows of WY.

TO MAKE UP
The first and last rows can now be grafted together to make an invisible join. Since grafting consists of making one row of stitches with a needle between the two rows of knitting, the row sequence will then be correct and match the other sections.
 Fold over the top of the skirt and insert elastic to fit the waist. Press the pleats into place.
 To finish the hem of the skirt, two rows of double crochet can be worked round the bottom. When pressed these will lie quite flat. Crab stitch is quite decorative. This is one row of double crochet worked in the usual way. The second row is worked backwards over the first. Do not turn the work round, but keep the same side facing and put the crochet hook into each stitch behind the first to work another double crochet.

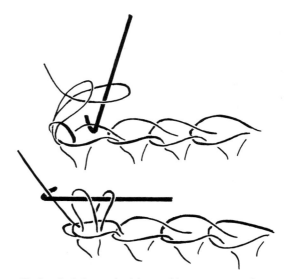

42 Crab stitch is worked by making one row of double crochet along the edge and, without turning the work round, crocheting another row backwards over the first. This makes a firm edge which will not roll

Variations on the circular skirt

1 Instead of having a wide band of straight rows between each section of holding position rows, knit only about two rows each side of the tuck and slip rows. The pleats will then be much nearer together, and since more sections will be needed to make the skirt wide enough at the hips, it will be more flared. The extra flare can be reduced by bringing more needles to holding position (say 20) on each row.

2 The amount of flare given to the skirt can be adjusted by the number of needles in holding position on each row. If fewer needles are brought out every two rows then more rows are knitted in the shaped section, making the skirt fuller, and of course the reverse is true – more needles to holding position, fewer rows and less flare. More needles can be put into holding position at the waist end, to give a smoother fit over the hips and then less in the lower half on every row to give more swing to the hem.

3 For a much more flared skirt, or if you wish to knit godets of a different colour, instead of knitting all the needles back to working position on one row, to begin the straight section, take back in the same sequence they were brought out, and a complete triangle of knitting is worked.

4 Quite an interesting design can be made if two rows of another colour are knitted on some of the short rows, randomly round the skirt. The rows will be of different lengths according to where they are introduced, or they can all be made the same length by knitting the same row on each section.

5 Fair Isle patterns or lace must be knitted on the straight sections so that the patterns are not interrupted.

The circular skirt lends itself to a variety of patterns and can form the basis for many different outfits in your wardrobe.

Panelled skirts

These are usually knitted in separate pieces from hem to waist. They can of course be knitted the opposite way, from the waist down, especially for children, where the garment may need to be lengthened at a later date.

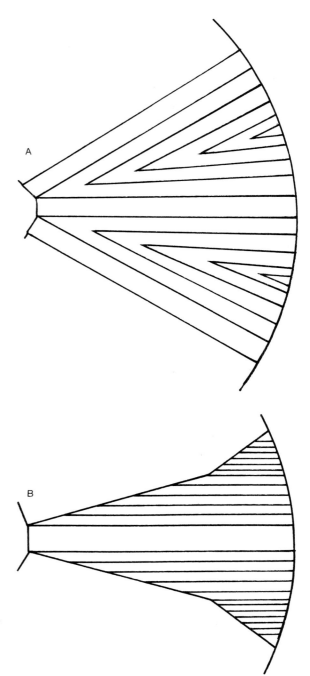

43 Variations on circular skirts

A By returning needles to working position in the same order that they were brought out to holding position, a much more flared skirt is made

B Fewer needles brought to holding position near the hem of the skirt makes it more flared in this section only

The panels are tapered into the waist at the sides, and since the slanting edge of each panel will be longer than the centre, as in dressmaking with a woven material, the bottom edge of the skirt is curved. If this shaping is not done on every panel the hem will droop where the pieces are stitched together. Put needles at each side into holding position over several rows so that more rows are knitted on the centre stitches. On a plain skirt this can be done immediately above the hem edge, but if there is a border pattern it cannot be distorted by putting needles into hold, so the shaping should be done after the border. If the skirt has an all-over pattern which will be spoilt by the shaping then it will have to be done right at the top before attaching the waistband, where it will be least noticeable. To work out the size of each panel the hip measurement (plus ease) should be divided by the number of panels required. If knitting a large size, extra pieces should be knitted to make a more comfortable fit. Five or six slightly narrower panels usually look better than stretching out four larger pieces. To give a flared look, the hem of the panel should be half as wide again as the hip. For example, for four panels to fit hips 96cm (38 in.) – actual size 101cm (40 in.) – hips = 101cm (40 in.) ÷ 4 = 25cm (10 in.). There is no need to work to fractions. The small amount lost at the hips will not be noticed, either round, down or up. Similarly at the hem: 25 + 12.5 = 37.5cm, so make this 38cm ($9\frac{3}{4} + 5 = 14\frac{3}{4}$ or 15 in.)

The hip level is taken as being 20cm (8 in.) below the waist, so all the decreasing up the sides of the skirt should be finished at this level. The skirt can then be knitted straight to the waist, which makes it easy to pull on. It will be gathered in with elastic.

A straight two-panelled skirt

This is the only skirt pattern given here that has a turned-up hem at the bottom. The skirt is lined with an iron-on fabric which stretches in the same way as the knitted fabric. While helping it to keep its shape, it gives a fine knitted fabric extra body. The hem can be turned up and stitched down to the lining material so that it does not show on the right side. Since this skirt is knitted in two almost straight pieces, there is only a small amount of

shaping with holding position rows and it is an ideal style to knit in an all-over pattern, such as a check or a plaid.

If you wish, knit it absolutely straight, sew darts in at the waist and insert a zip in the side seam as you would with a woven material.

This pattern uses two colours, each in a 2-ply equivalent thickness. As the plaid design is an all-over pattern and the floats are being carried across the back of the fabric, the end product is a knitted fabric equivalent in thickness to a 4-ply. 2-ply lambswool may be used, or any other combination of fine industrial yarns which gives the same weight.

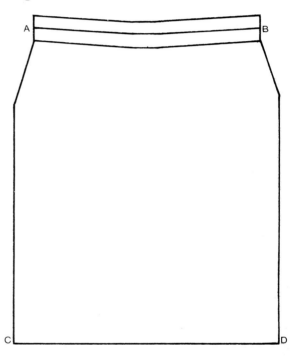

44 Diagram for the two-panelled Fair Isle skirt

AB =	50	53	59	cm
	$19\frac{3}{4}$	$20\frac{3}{4}$	$23\frac{1}{4}$	in.
AC =	66			cm
	26			in.

Size   Length 66cm (26 in.)

| *To fit hips* | 86 to 91 | 96 to 101 | 106 to 111cm |
| | 34 to 36 | 38 to 40 | 42 to 44 in. |

Materials   2 cones 2/30 acrylic yarn from Nantiago Homecrafts. 2 cones of 2/30 acrylic yarn from Atkinsons Yarns. Two strands of each colour used together. 1 metre (yard) fusible nylon from Metropolitan Sewing Machines

Tension   34 stitches and 36 rows to 10cm (4 in.) at MT approx 4.

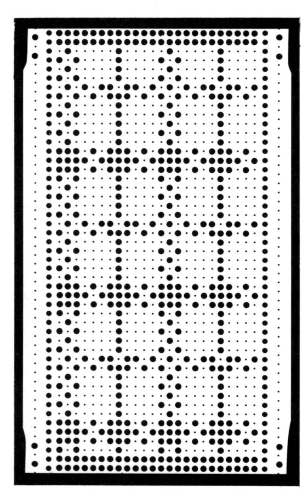

45 Punchcard for the plaid design of the skirt. A matching jacket, reversing the colours, would complement the skirt

Insert card punched out as shown in fig. 45, and lock onto row 1.
Using WY (something fairly fine) cast on 174 182 200 sts.
Knit a few rows. Change to *one* strand of grey 2/30 (main colour).
MT–2. Knit 12 rows.

Knit 1 row at MT and join in the second strand of grey yarn, running it in through the same tension wire on the mast.
Lock onto punchcard and knit selecting row.
RC 000.
Set carr to knit Fair Isle/multicolour and join in the 2 strands of the second colour of 2/30 in feeder B.
Release card.
Continue to knit in pattern to RC 166 (*hip level*).
Decrease 1 st at each end of the next and every following 15 rows until there are 160 170 190 sts.
Knit to RC 236. On next 10 rows push 1 needle to HP opposite carr.
Cancel all patterning and knit 1 row in grey only, across all needles.
RC 247.
Remove 1 strand of grey yarn, knit 1 row.
Change tension to MT–2 and knit 12 rows. Take off on several rows of WY.

TO MAKE UP
When both pieces have been knitted the side seams should be sewn together by hand using mattress stitch, carefully matching the pattern.
   Iron on the nylon lining to fit, and turn the hems over top and bottom and catch down onto it. Thread elastic through the top.
   You may use any other suitable all-over punch-card pattern for this skirt.

Waistbands

Sometimes it is not practicable to use the quick, folded-over waistband that has been used in these patterns. For example, if on a sideways-knitted skirt all the needles have been used and the skirt is still not long enough, then the waistband can be added at the top to give the extra length. Also, if the fabric of the skirt is bulky, perhaps because you have worked it by weaving, or a very knobbly yarn has been used, then to fold the top over will make an uncomfortable lump. Here are several methods of making a waistband.

1 *Using slip stitch*   This is an excellent method, since it is much less bulky than any other. The casing is finished on the machine without having to pick up stitches. The only disadvantage is that on a skirt which has the knit side as the right side, the waistband made like this will have the purl stitches showing.

Pick up the stitches from half of the top of the skirt, right side facing. Knit one row at main tension and insert card 1 (alternate needles selected). Lock on row 1 and keep it locked. Knit the row to select the pattern needles. Set the carriage to slip/part and knit 16–20 rows. Only the alternate needles will knit. Knit slowly and watch that the stitches all knit properly and do not push off the needles. Set the machine for stocking stitch and knit one row at a loose tension. Cast off loosely.

Alternatively, to give a neater finish on the back of the work, knit several rows and take off onto waste yarn. The last row knitted in the main yarn can then be caught down on the back through every stitch. It will cover the top of the skirt where the stitches were picked up.

This method of making a casing using slip stitch can also be used at the sleeves to gather them in with elastic or ribbon, at the waist on the

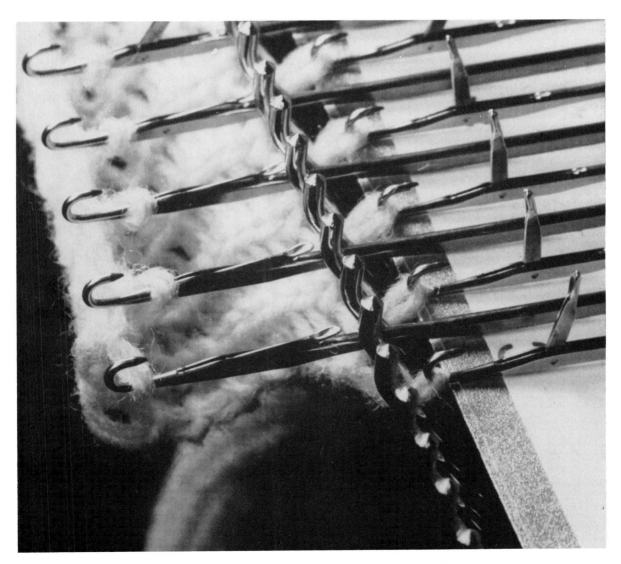

46 Slip-stitch waistband showing the stitches being knitted on the forward needles, producing a loop of fabric. On the next row knitted across all needles this will close up making the casing for the waistband

inside of a dress for threading a cord, or at the neck of a jumper to thread a cord or ribbon. Other ways of using this stitch are given in chapter 9 as a patterning method.

2 *Picking up the stitches from the top of the skirt, in two halves*   From the tension square, estimate the number of stitches required to pull the skirt up over the hips since the skirt must stretch to this.

Pick up the stitches evenly along half the top of the skirt. On a four-panelled skirt you will need to join two panels together first, at least for about 5cm (2 in.). Knit the band at MT−1 for a slightly firmer fit. Knit the number of rows you require, for a 4-ply yarn between 12 and 20 depending on the depth. Knit one loose row to give a good fold, and knit the same number for the second half. Pick up the stitches from the first row of the band onto the needles. Change to MT+2, knit one row. Knit one more as loosely as possible, and cast off round sinker pins. (This cast-off edge must be loose. If it feels tight then the stitches will eventually wear as the skirt is pulled on and off.)

If you wish to attach a lining to the skirt, then before casting off knit 4–6 rows straight, at the looser tension. This will give you a flap to which the lining can be sewn.

3 *Knitting a separate band*   The method for this is the same as (2), except that you start with waste yarn and sew it onto the skirt afterwards. It can be attached quickly using a sewing machine.

Cast on with waste yarn. Change to main yarn and knit the band. Pick up the first row of stitches above the waste yarn and knit 6–8 rows in main yarn. Take off on waste yarn. Pin the six rows to the top of the skirt, right sides together, and stitch together on the machine (or by hand, making sure you catch every stitch) using a small zigzag if you have one, or a long straight stitch. Do two rows of stitching as close as possible to the double layer. Unravel the waste yarn – there is no need to cast off the last row of knitting as it will be secured by the machine knitting.

Hems and edgings

These can be used not only on skirts, but also on pocket tops, necklines, collar edges, etc.

Usually it is necessary to do something to the bottom of the skirt to prevent the fabric from rolling. It is best to avoid putting an actual turned-up hem on a skirt because so often it is difficult to make it lie flat. If you do knit a hem, *never* turn it up and pick up the stitches on the machine. Always catch the stitches down by hand afterwards. This way there is never any danger of making a tight row which distorts the hem. Here are a few other ideas.

1 *Rope edging*   Using the three-pronged transfer tool, place three stitches from the hem edge right side facing, onto three needles. Knit six rows on these three stitches, pick up three stitches from the edge, next to the first three, and place them on the same needles. Knit six rows. Repeat until you have been right round the hem. Stitch the last three stitches down to match. The number of rows knitted can be varied: fewer will give a smoother edging, more will give a more looped, rope-like appearance. This edging can also be used on pocket tops and round collars or cuffs.

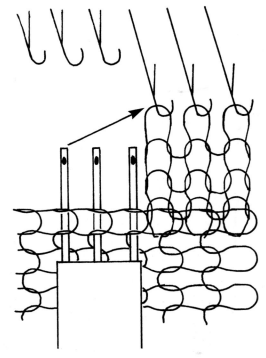

47 Rope edging made on the side of a piece of knitting, or hem. Insert the three-pronged transfer tool into the knitting and place the stitches onto the needles. Knit several rows, and repeat along the length required, using the same three needles throughout

2 *Braid sewn round the hem* A shell edging which folds over on itself can be knitted quite quickly, but it needs to be sewn on at both sides of the knitting.

Cast on by hand over eight needles arranged as follows: 11–1–1–1–11.
             *   *

Knit 4 rows.
Pull needles marked * to HP by hand. Knit 4 rows.
Push needles back to UWP. Knit 4 rows.
Repeat last eight rows for the length required.
The tucked stitches pull in at the sides making the centre stitches bulge to make the shell, and also make the braid fold itself neatly in half, which is easy to sew onto the hem.

3 If you have a ribber, a very small hem of about four rows can be made at the bottom and then pressed out so that it does not gather in the bottom edge.

4 To make a scalloped edge that will lie flat, cast on using the e-wrap to make a closed edge. Knit two rows. Select needles at regular intervals along the row. Work out which to use so that they divide evenly into the number of stitches you are using, e.g. every 15th or 20th needle along the row, and bring them out to holding position. Knit six rows, taking care that the stitches each side of these in holding position are knitted properly – they tend to push up off the needles. Knit one row across all needles and take the work off onto waste yarn, or onto the garter bar. Turn it over and replace onto the same needles. Bring the same needles as before out to holding position and knit four rows. Set the machine to knit all needles and continue to knit.

5 A small scallop edge can be made without turning the work over if the needles selected for holding position are nearer together, about every fourth stitch.

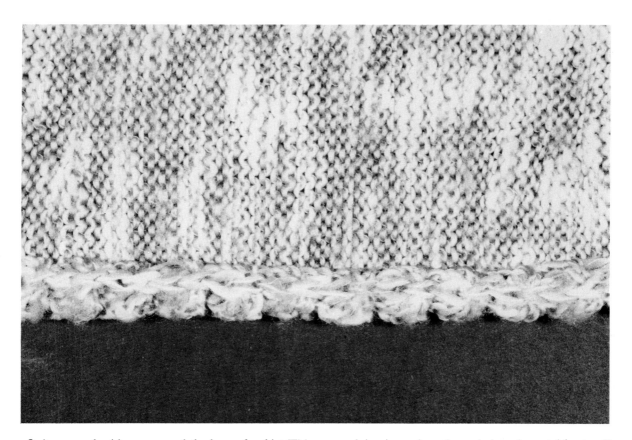

48 A narrow braid sewn round the hem of a skirt. This same edging is used on the mohair waistcoat (chapter 6)

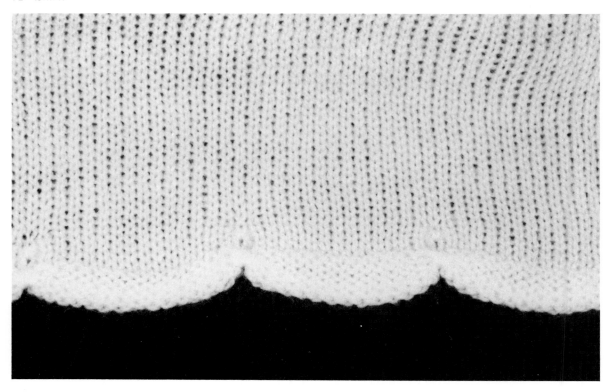

49 Scalloped hem on a skirt. The work is turned round above the edging to face the opposite way to make a hem that will not curl

Weaving

Weaving is a stitch that is unique to machine knitting. It makes a very firm pattern fabric with no floats and is ideal for cut-and-sew.

It is made by knitting with one yarn, and a second one is caught in on the surface (purl side) of the knitting. The weaving brushes at the front of the sinker plate are either lowered or screwed into place according to your instruction book.

The knitting yarn can be cheap as it is not very noticeable on the right side. However, consider its colour – a dark or light background will change the appearance.

For weaving use Aran, mohair and chunky yarns which are too thick to knit on the standard-gauge machine. Because the weaving yarn travels straight across the needles, and does not curve round to make the stitch shape, much less length is used than would be needed to actually knit with it. So a more expensive yarn can be used for weaving.

Hand-knitting yarns need not be rewound. It is not necessary to thread the yarn through the yarn break, and the balls can be laid on the floor and fed into the machine by hand. They do not unwind as quickly as the yarn used for knitting. For machines whose needles are selected to upper working position by the punchcard, the weaving yarn is laid across the front needles on each row. Do not hold the yarn tightly but allow it to be taken up slightly by the stitches. For Knitmaster machines the weaving yarn must be hooked over the yarn guides at the leading edge of the sinker plate. At the end of the row it must be taken out and hooked through the opposite end.

The best embossed effect of weaving is seen if the weaving yarn is thicker than the knitting yarn. However, a very flat, firm fabric is made by using the same weight of yarn to knit and weave.

Several ends of fine yarn can be used together to achieve the thickness desired for weaving. This is a good way of using up some smaller cones.

The weaving yarn tends to push the stitches apart slightly, so although the tension of the knitting yarn need not be set at much more than the tension normal for that yarn, you will find that the tension swatch will indicate fewer stitches per 10cm (4 in.) than stocking stitch.

Some weaving variations

1 A pattern card which produces long floats can be used to make fringes. The long floats are cut in the centre and allowed to hang freely. This reveals more of the background knitting yarn. The weaving yarn must be securely anchored over two or three stitches so that it will not pull out. More silky yarns may need greater areas of weaving to secure them but they will hang well.

2 Another way of patterning with long floats on a woven fabric is to hook them up onto needles on the row above, producing a new range of patterns. the loops can be latched through one another for several rows, or looped up individually onto different needles on every row.

3 Knitting at a tight tension will make the knitting contract more when released from the needles and the weaving yarn will loop up between the stitches. This makes a rather stiff material suitable for coats perhaps, or even rugs.

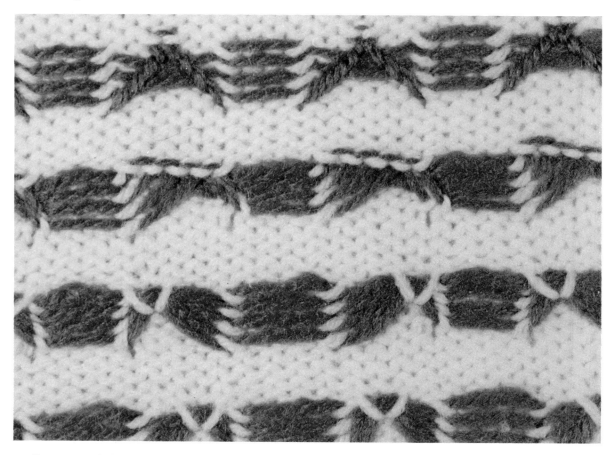

50 Patterns made by weaving with long floats. *Top of sample* Floats have been latched through one another and the last one hooked onto the centre needle   *Second row* Each float has been looped onto a different needle all on the same row   *Bottom rows* All floats have been hooked up onto the same needle at one side

Waistcoat woven with mohair

To fit	81	86	91	96	101	cm
	34	36	38	40	42	in.

Materials Knitting yarn 150–180gm Atkinsons 2/30 acrylic used double. Weaving yarn 3 × 50-gm balls Jarol Romantica mohair for all sizes

Tension 24 sts and 40 rows to 10cm (4 in.) at MT approx 8

PATTERN NOTES

1 If the weaving pattern being used has a definite right way up, the punchcard must be turned round and inserted into the machine upside down for the back in the middle of the shoulder shaping. On an electronic machine set to reverse. The punchcard pattern in fig. 52 is similar both ways – it will not need to be reversed.

2 These are loose-fitting armholes, so there is room to add an armband instead of binding with braid if you prefer.

Insert card into machine and lock on first row.

Knit 2 pockets first. Using 2/30 double, cast on 34 sts.

Knit 54 rows at MT.

Engage card with next row. Release it and knit-weave the last 5 rows of the pocket. Take off on WY.

LEFT FRONT

Using WY cast on 58 60 62 64 70 sts.

Knit a few rows, change to MY and MT − 2. Knit 10 rows.

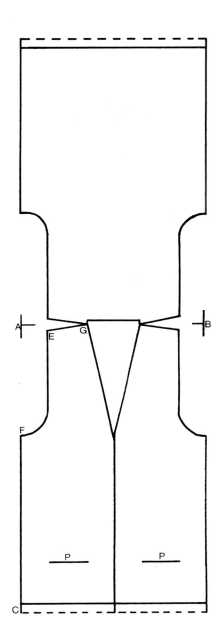

51 Woven waistcoat, shoulders joined on the machine and knitted from front hem over to the back hem

AB =	43	45	48	50	53	cm
	17	17¾	19	19¾	21	in.
AF =	20	20.5	22	22.5	23	cm
	7¾	8	8¾	8¾	9	in.
FC =	35	36	36	37.5	38.5	cm
	13¼	14¼	14¼	14¾	15¼	in.
EG =	10	10.5	11	12	12.5	cm
	4	4¼	4¼	4¾	5	in.

P = pocket postion approx 15 cm
(6 in.) from bottom

Engage card on row 1 and knit the row. Release card.
RC 000.
Change to MT. Knit in weaving pattern to RC 60.
Using spare length of yarn cast off 34 sts in centre.
Replace sts from one of pocket linings onto empty needles, continue to knit in pattern to RC 140 145 145 150 154.

Shape armholes and sloping front
Cast off 12 12 14 14 14 sts at beg of next row.
Cast off 1 st at beg of next row and every 4th row following, to shape front.
Cast off 1 st at armhole edge at beg of next 4 alt rows (40 42 44 46 52 sts).
Continuing in pattern, dec at front edge only on every 4th row to 24 26 28 30 32 sts.
Knit to RC 220 228 234 240 246.

Shape shoulder and back neck
Push 6 sts to HP at shoulder edge on next 3 alt rows. Push the 6 needles back to WP on next 3 alt rows, keeping pattern correct.
RC 236 236 246 252 258.
Take off on WY.

RIGHT FRONT
Cast on to left of 0 starting at needle number 22.
Knit right front to match, reversing shapings. Do not remove from machine. Lock punchcard.

BACK
Leaving 42 needles in centre of machine empty, replace sts from left front onto machine, beg with needle number 22 to left of 0.
Using a spare length of yarn cast on over the centre needles for back neck.
Keeping it locked, engage punchcard.
Make sure all needles are back in B position. Set carr to slip and take it across needle bed empty to select needles for first weaving row.
RC 000.
Continue in pattern to RC 82 82 90 92 107 rows.

Shape armholes
Inc 1 st at beg of next 8 rows.
Inc by e-wrapping 12 12 14 14 14 sts at beg of next 2 rows (118 120 122 128 130 sts).
Continue in pattern to RC 224 228 234 240 246.
Cancel punchcard and cut off weaving yarn.
Lower weaving brushes. Knit 10 rows in 2 × 2/30 only for hem. Take off on WY.

TO MAKE UP

Stitch up the side seams.

Make a braid to bind the front edges, armholes and pocket tops. Use a shell braid (see chapter 5), or a plain bias strip:

Cast on at the extreme left of the needle bed, over 10 stitches.
MT − 2, knit 2 rows. COR.
Inc 1 st at right, knit 1 row.
Dec 1 st at left, knit 1 row.
Repeat these last two rows until the braid is long enough, replacing it on needles on the left.

A striped braid can be knitted like this. The stripes will run diagonally across the knitting when it is sewn on to the garment, like the cowl collar in chapter 4.

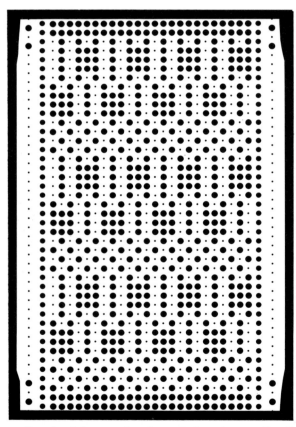

52 Punchard for weaving the mohair waistcoat. Small block pattern produced by weaving ties in with the pattern on the plaid skirt. The two are shown worn together in colour plate 8

Pattern for woven crossover jacket

To fit	81–91	94 –101	103–106	cm
	32–36	36½– 40	40½– 44	in.

Materials   For knitting, one strand 2/24 lambs-wool and one strand 2/30 acrylic, used together (approx a fine 3-ply yarn) 400gm. Approx 350gm for weaving Aran-thickness Poodle from Uppingham Yarns

Tension   Using card 1 from basic pack (see fig. 54), alt needles selected, 24 sts and 42 rows to 10cm (4 in.) at MT approx 8

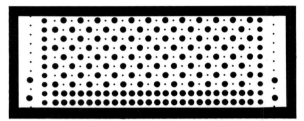

53 Punchcard used for the woven jacket, alternate needles selected. This is card 1 in most of the basic sets. Punchout card as shown for 36 rows

PATTERN NOTES

1 The weaving method of casting on is used because a length of yarn is threaded through the first row of stitches. This can be drawn up to fit snugly inside the cuff, and stitched down. Lower or fit the weaving brushes. Bring alternate needles to D or E position and thread the carriage. Pull an extra length of yarn below the carriage and lay it across the needles. Hold the end. Take the carriage across the needles and the first row of stitches is secure.

2 It can be a slow process to use the holding position when weaving. The needles need to be placed back into working position with the stitches behind the latches. The quickest way is to knit them back, thus:

Lock the card.
Cancel all the patterning mechanism. Weaving brushes can be left in WP. Set carr so that needles will knit back on next row to WP.
Unravel row just knitted, keeping all sts in front of latches.

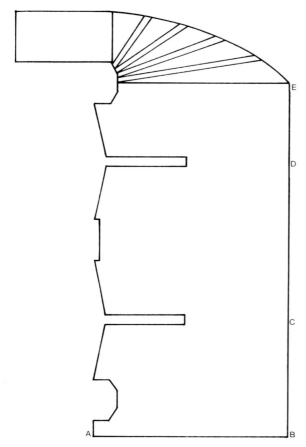

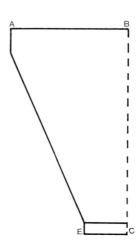

54 Sideways-knitted woven jacket. Extra rows are knitted at the underarm section to make the larger sizes

Body		cm	*Sleeve*				cm
AB = 65		cm	AB = 33	34.5	36		cm
	25½	in.		13	13½	14	in.
BC = 39		cm	EC = 18.5	19	21		cm
	15¼	in.		7¼	7½	8¼	in.
CD = 53		cm	CB = 40	41	43		cm
	21	in.		15¾	16	17	in.
DE = 29		cm					
	11½	in.					

All needles in WP.

Lock carr onto punchcard, set it to *slip* and take carr back across needles to side where the yarn is. The needles are now selected for next row. Turn RC back 2 rows. Release punchcard, thread up machine and continue to knit/weave.

This method can be used if making a woven sideways-knitted skirt, where all the needles are taken back to working position on one row (see pleated skirt pattern, chapter 5). For a garment like this try knitting with one strand of 2/24 and weaving with a 4-ply yarn, or a double knitting and a fairly large tension. The skirt will not then be so stiff and thick that it will not drape well. There is no danger of a woven skirt dropping in wear as the fabric is so stable across the row.

3 *Fringe* Cast on over needles 46–40 to left of centre o and over needles 40–46 to the right. Bring out two needles in centre of bed and knit one row with the punchcard locked. Release card and set to knit elongated pattern. Set carr to tuck. This gives more strands of yarn across the bed for the length knitted to make a fuller fringe.

Knit to RC 120, or until it is long enough to go across the end of the 'scarf'. Release the two centre stitches from the needles and cast off at each end.

Sew the fringe edges to each side of the end of the scarf and cut the strands through the middle.

4 The knitting yarn can be any 4-ply or equivalent thickness. Three strands of 2/30 in contrasting colours will add variety to the knitting.

A fine bouclé 2-ply, and one strand of 2/30, will give some texture to the knitting. A Shetland wool is not recommended because it breaks easily. However, a Shetland-and-nylon mixture is very good, as it is stronger and warm.

5 The yarn used for weaving should be about the

thickness of a hand-knitting Aran. It could also be plied handspun – perhaps mixed greys and cream, or two or three thinner yarns run in together.

BODY

Commence at the right front. Lower weaving brushes or screw them into position.
Using knitting yarn, cast on 156 sts by weaving method.
MT − 2. Knit 10 rows.
Change to MT. Engage punchcard, lock on row 1.
Knit 1 row.
Release punchcard and begin weaving with thicker yarn.
Knit 20 rows. COL.

Shape neck
Cast off 10 sts at left. Dec 1 st at neck edge at beg of next 10 alt rows.
RC 40 (136 sts).
Knit 24 rows.
Inc 1 st at neck edge at beg of next 10 alt rows.
RC 84.
Cast on 10 sts at beg of next row at neck edge (156 sts).

Shape shoulder
Knit 80 rows, at same time dec 1 st at left side on every 12th row 6 times.
RC 164 (150 sts).

Shape left armhole
Cast off 60 sts at left.
Knit 10 20 26 rows.
RC 174 184 190.

BACK

Cast on 60 sts at left (150 sts).

Shape shoulder
Knit 80 rows, inc 1 st at beg of 6th and every following 12th row 6 times.
RC 254 264 270 (140 sts).
Cast off 4 sts at left edge for back neck.
Knit 64 rows.
RC 318 328 334.
Cast on 4 sts.

Shape shoulder
Knit 80 rows, dec 1 st at beg of every 12th row 6 times.
RC 398 408 414 (150 sts).

Shape right armhole
Cast off 60 sts at left.

RIGHT FRONT

Knit 10 20 26 rows.
RC 408 428 440.
Cast on 60 sts.

Shape shoulder
Knit 80 rows inc 1 st on 6th and every following 12th row.
RC 488 508 520 (156 sts).

Shape neck
Cast off 10 sts at beg of next row on left.
Dec 1 st at beg of next 10 alt rows at left side (136 sts).

Shape bottom edge
Knit 1 row. Dec 1 st at bottom (right) edge at beg of every alt row, until only 40 sts remain.
RC 000 COL.
* Still dec at right and always wrapping the inside needle in HP, bring 12 needles at left to HP on next row then 5 on every alt row until only 5 needles are left. Return all needles to WP.**
(See note 2.) Knit 8 rows.
RC 48 (106 sts).
Repeat from * to **. With 3 needles left, knit 5 rows straight, then inc 1 st left on next 2 alt rows, to shape neck.
RC 88.
Repeat from * to **. With 4 sts left, knit 8 rows, inc 1 st at left on all alt rows.
RC 122.
*** Always wrapping inside needle in HP, bring 10 needles at left to HP on next row, then 3 on every alt row. Return all needles to WP ****. Knit 8 rows, inc 1 st at left on straight rows 4 times.
RC 164.
Neck shaping is now complete.
Repeat from *** to **** twice. RC 186.
Knit 80 rows straight, and cast off.

SLEEVES

Using weaving method cast on 90 95 102 sts.
Knit 10 rows at MT − 2.
Change to MT and connect onto the locked punchcard.

Knit 1 row.

Continue to weave. Knit 10 rows.

Inc 1 st at beg of next 2 rows and every 3rd and 4th row following until there are 160 165 172 sts.

Continue to knit straight to RC 160 166 166.

Cast off around sinker pins, or take off onto WY.

TO MAKE UP

Join shoulder seams.

Sew in sleeves and join sleeve seam. Turn up hems.

BRAID FOR EDGING

Using knitting yarn cast on 12 sts. Lock punchcard on row 1 and knit 1 row at MT.

Set carriage for tuck.

Release card and knit sufficient length to go from the end of the 'scarf' at left side front to bottom of right edge – approx 208 cm (82 in.).

Stitch this on round the edge, stretching slightly to ease it round the curve. Turn it over to the back and catch down inside. Make a fringe and stitch to the end of the 'scarf'.

NECKBAND

With wrong side facing pick up approx 180 sts round neck edge onto needles.

Lock punchcard and knit 1 row MT to select needles.

Release card and set carr to tuck.

Knit 4 rows.

Push 1 needle to HP next to carr, set to hold. On next 24 rows gradually reduce tension to MT − 4. RC 30.

Bring 1 needle to WP at beg of every row until all needles are knitting, at the same time gradually inc to MT.

RC 54.

Knit 4 rows in tuck pattern, then 2 rows st st at MT.

Take off on WY and stitch down on right side through each st.

INNER EDGE OF 'SCARF'

Pick up 50 sts along edge and cast on 1 extra st at neck end for mattress st.

Knit 1 row MT. Lock punchcard and knit 1 row. Release card and set to tuck.

Reduce tension to MT − 2 and knit 14 rows in tuck pattern. Change to MT and knit 2 rows. Take off on WY.

Turn to right side, and stitch down to match neck edging. Mattress-stitch braid and neckband together.

A more traditional shape

The same measurements can be used as for the crossover jacket to make a coat which fastens at the centre front. Begin with the left front and knit across the back and right front in one piece, casting off for the armholes in the same way. A turned-back hem on the centre fronts can have buttons and buttonholes, or a zip. A hood can be added using the measurements from the hood of the handspun coat (chapter 11).

This is a quickly made garment. There are no side seams or shapings. The sleeves can be finished on the machine by picking up the side seams of the sleeve onto the needles and casting off both stitches together.

CHAPTER 7

Multicolour knitting

The name 'Fair Isle' has become synonymous with colour patterns in knitting and it was on the Shetland island of Fair Isle that the coloured and stranded patterns were first developed. The natural colours of the Shetland fleeces, which range from creamy white through browns and greys to black, were used and the wools were dyed with lichens, to give a variety of fast colours.

The shape of the traditional Fair Isle jumper is square, with no shaping for the armholes, offering more scope for decoration. The sleeves were knitted short to keep them dry. The stranding of the yarn across the back makes the knitting thicker and warmer, and although the colours may be changed many times in the complete pattern, only two colours are knitted in any one row. The modern machine which knits two colours, with the strands on the back, makes a true copy of the traditional knitting.

The floats which are taken across the back of the fabric between the selected needles reduce the elasticity of the knitting because the straight strands do not have the same 'give' as the curved knitted stitch shape. To compensate for this it is necessary to increase the stitch size. Increase the tension by two whole numbers more than normally used for the same yarn in stocking stitch. If you are knitting a band of Fair Isle on an otherwise plain stocking stitch garment, for the patterned rows increase the tension for those rows only. This will keep the width of the knitting the same as the plain area, but the length in rows will be different, so if it is a band of more than about 20 rows then another tension swatch must be made, in order to calculate how many fewer rows are needed to obtain the correct length.

Dealing with the floats

These are a problem if they are more than five or six stitches long. If you are knitting a garment for a child, choose a design with short floats or anchor them well, particularly on the sleeves, where small fingers may become entangled.

The following are some of the ways of dealing with the floats.

1 They can be held down in place by an extra length of yarn. This is e-wrapped round a needle at the side of the area to anchor it, and every few rows it is taken across the floats and looped onto a needle. There is then a vertical yarn crossing the horizontal threads. For each pattern repeated across the garment a separate thread must be used.

2 Loop up the float onto a needle immediately above on each row. Do not knit it through the stitch or it will show on the right side. Pick up loops from both the patterning and the background yarns.

3 If there are long floats on rows above one another they can be left for several rows then latched up, the last loop being hooked up onto the needle as in (1).

4 Cover the area of floats with either a piece of fine knitting or a lining fabric. Vilene Supershape is a manmade interfacing which can be ironed onto the knitting and which stretches sideways but not lengthways. This can be used to cover small areas.

1 A quartet of raglans.   *Back left* Extra-wide motifs of planets on an all-in-one V-neck raglan jumper. Stripes knitted between body and sleeves on the holding position needles   *Back right* Winding pattern made on the holding position needles before knitting the all-in-one raglan and picking up the neckband   *Front right* Narrow cable section added to the front of a jumper with wide shell edging on the raglan shaping   *Front left* Plain all-in-one raglan sleeves, with three wide-motif dachshunds

2 Sideways-knitted raglan jumper with a cowl collar knitted diagonally. Teamed with a shadow pleated skirt

3 Right A yoked jumper with traditional style of patterning, colours graduated through three shades, teamed with a circular pleated skirt. The beret and gloves are made from the patterns in chapter 3

4 Opposite Cats and mice in close proximity!

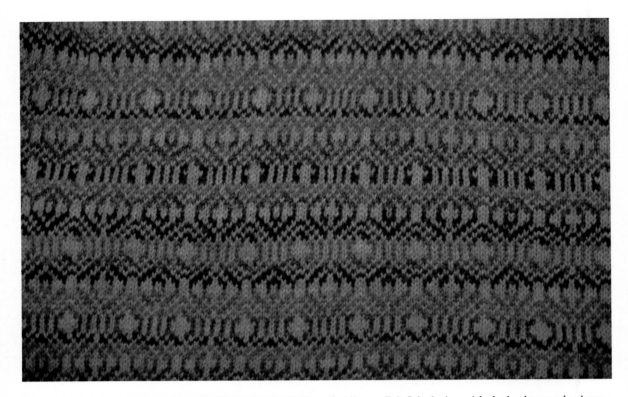

5 All-over Fair Isle design with the background colours changed every two, four and six rows

6 Left The anemone design with three colours in a row at the centre of the flowers, knitted onto a jumper with narrow shell-raglan shaping

7 Opposite Left Woven mohair jacket waistcoat with braid edging, worn with the two-panelled plaid skirt. The wall hanging has individually made flowers sewn to the background

8 Opposite Right Woven crossover jacket

9 OPPOSITE Various cable designs used to pattern a man's jumper

10 ABOVE Slip stitch ruched pattern jacket. Background of rainbow-dyed yarns

11 Simple overtop made in slip stitch. The colours are carried from one horizontal coloured section to the next to give vertical stripes in three colours

12 Hooded coat woven by using alternate needles to accommodate the thick plied handspun in three colours. Alpaca, camel hair and mohair

13 Two garments in handspun wool. Slipover designed from the basic block, and made from yarns dyed with elderberries for the Regine Faust punchcard design. Waistcoat knitted from Jacob's fleece using traditional Fair Isle patterns

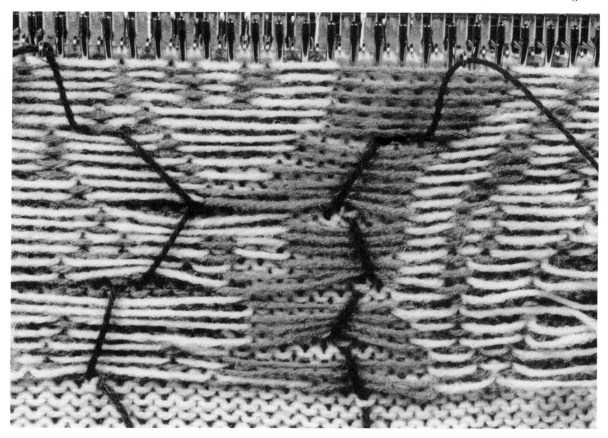

55 Using a separate thread to hold down the floats in Fair Isle knitting. Loop it into the needle, every few rows. Do not allow it to knit through

Designing punchcards

When making your own designs it is important to remember that the knitted stitch is not square. It is one-third longer than it is wide. Figure 56 shows a design on a punchcard, and fig. 57 shows the same design when it is knitted. In order to finish with equal-sided blocks which are six stitches wide, it is necessary to punch out eight rows of holes. On the punchcard this looks rectangular, but when knitted the squat shape of the stitch produces a square. The lower design is six holes (stitches) wide and six holes (rows) deep. This is not square when knitted.

So when designing something like the mice or cats of the patterns, which are roughly square, and 20–22 stitches wide, the animals need to be drawn about 29 rows long. Packs of punchcard design paper with rectangles of the correct proportion can be bought to draw your designs before transferring them to the cards or sheets. The patterns will look 'right' on the paper but, when punched on the cards, will look elongated.

Two rows of overlap holes must be punched at each end of the card if it is to revolve continuously. Make sure that the pattern does actually repeat correctly, finishing at the top of the card with the row which fits immediately onto the bottom row. Do not punch out the last row of the last pattern if it is also the first row of the next one. It may be necessary to repeat the pattern two or more times to give a long enough piece of card to revolve in the machine (at least 36 rows).

The row which can be seen when the card is inserted into the machine, marked row 1 on the prepared cards, is not the first row to be knitted. It has to go far enough down into the slot for the machine to read the pattern. On the Brother and Toyota machines it is seven rows below this; on the Knitmaster it is five rows below; and Singer machines knit four rows below. So if you wish to start knitting in the middle of a card, e.g. at row 36, position the card so that row 36 is the first row to be seen, then click it round manually counting 7 (5 or 4 depending on the make of machine) until row number 43 (41 or 40) is the next one to be seen. It will now begin knitting the pattern from row 36.

If the design is one in which every two rows knit exactly the same stitches, then card length and punching time can be saved by punching out only one row of each two. Set the card to elongate, so that it knits every row punched twice before moving on.

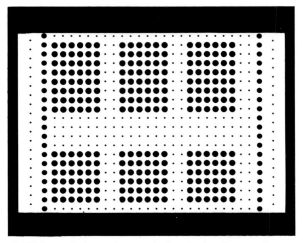

56 This card shows how a design looks elongated when punched onto the card. The knitted stitch is about one-third wider than it is long

57 How the rectangle on the punchcard looks square when knitted, and the square is knitted into a squashed shape

Motifs

On punchcard machines the motifs can only be placed within each 24-stitch block of needles, or halfway across two sets of 24 stitches, if the pattern is punched out with the two halves of the motif at each side of the punchcard (see sleeves of 'mice' jumper). The motifs can be positioned anywhere on the garment, but if the position required does not fit into the 24-stitch repeats then the knitting itself must be re-aligned on the machine so that the motif will knit where you want it.

This problem does not apply to electronic machines. The motif can be programmed to knit anywhere on the needle bed without the restrictions of the repeats of the punchcard.

Most machines now have cams which are placed onto the needle bed to select the needles for the motif; see your instruction manual.

If the motif has straight sides the floats will pull the knitting away from the main garment, leaving an ugly gap in the stitches beside the pattern. This does not show up so much when the motif has an irregular edge, but it is advisable to wrap the motif edges to avoid this separation from the rest of the knitting. Join in a separate length of the background yarn at each side of the motif by e-wrapping it round a needle to one side. Do not allow the machine to knit through the one on the needle. On every row, at the side nearest to the carriage, take the binding yarn over the end patterning needle *and* the adjacent needle which is knitted in the background colour, then knit the row. The two edge needles are joined by the separate strand of yarn. This technique can be used on all machines.

Knitting wider motifs

To knit a motif which is more than 24 stitches wide, such as the planet (fig. 58), the extra needles are selected by hand. The centre of the pattern is punched out onto the card, and the additional needles required are charted onto paper. Note each row as you knit so that you don't select the same row twice, or miss one out.

The motif cams are placed onto the needle bed as before, or the needles to each side of the selected 24 stitches are pushed back, then the extra needles at each side are brought forward to upper working position by hand. They will knit in the second colour.

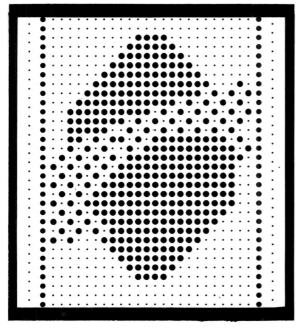

58 Punchcard for the centre of the planet

59 Chart showing the needles to pull forward by hand each side of the needles selected by the punchcard

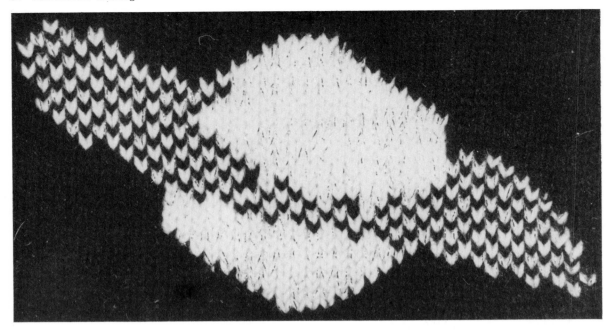

60 The complete motif

The dachshund (figs. 61 and 62) is another example of a wide motif, but since the extra stitches for the head and tail are so few it is easier to mark the stitches to be selected at each side onto the punchcard.

Mark the card so that the head and tail stitches are the correct number of rows up the card. The dotted line on fig. 61 shows the edge of the punchcard. This card is marked to be knitted on a Brother machine – eight rows before the actual marks.

A single motif can be added to a stocking stitch garment without knitting a separate tension swatch for it. It will not alter the overall tension of the knitting, and of course it is impossible to increase the tension for the motif without increasing the tension all across the row.

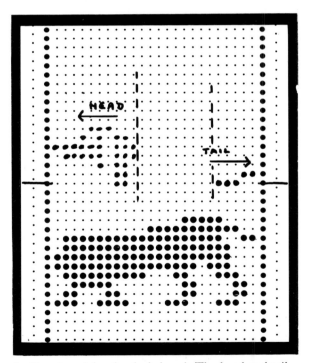

61 Punchcard for the dachshund. The head and tail are knitted outside the 24 stitches and are marked on this card to be knitted at the appropriate row eight rows above that seen on the card (for a Brother machine). Dotted line shows the edge of the 24 centre stitches

62 The complete dachshund

Cut-and-sew

This technique is useful for the necks of Fair Isle jumpers as it speeds up the construction. The section to be cut out can be marked as you knit, or tack round the shape afterwards. Press the work to set the stitches, making it easier to cut the piece.

Alter the pressure on the sewing machine foot so that it presses lightly onto the knitting. Too much pressure will make the fabric stretch as you sew, resulting in a loose, wavy edge. If this does happen, thread a length of fine knit-in elastic along the edge and pull it up so that the side is eased back into shape. This can be left in position after finishing the seam.

Use a polyester thread and sew two lines of narrow zigzag or serpentine stitch round the area to be cut. Use a fairly long stitch. If you cannot do a zigzag, then use a very large stitch. If you have to do it by hand, either use matching yarn or polyester thread and back-stitch round the shape to be cut out. If you feel nervous about cutting through the knitting, a very narrow strip of iron-on interfacing can be stuck around the edge and the stitching and cutting done through this.

Cut-and-sew can be used on any knitting. When working on a complicated pattern it is simpler to cut out the armholes and necklines afterwards. The front of a jacket can be knitted in one piece and cut in half up the centre. This ensures that both sides match exactly. This method is useful when knitting with several different strands of 2/30 yarns, which may give a somewhat random colouring. Leave the centre stitch out of work. This gives a guide for sewing straight up each side of it with the machine. The ladder can then be cut.

If you cut a knitted fabric without sewing it first it must be well pressed to stabilize it. Use sharp scissors to reduce fraying and handle carefully.

You have made your own length of material. If you had bought it in a shop you would cut it, even a knitted fabric, without hesitation – so don't be afraid to cut your knitting.

Ladies' mouse jumper in 2-ply lambswool

To fit	81	86	91	97	101	106	cm
	32	34	36	38	40	42	in.

Materials   Main colour 200–250gm 2/16 lambswool from Simply Shetland. Contrast 100–130gm lambswool

Tension   36 sts and 44 rows to 10cm (4 in.) MT at approx 7, measured over washed Fair Isle pattern

PATTERN NOTES

1 Punch out the card as shown in fig. 64. When the full length of the card has been knitted, take it out and turn it round so that the mice are facing the opposite way. The cats can be used for this garment if you prefer, or alternate cats and mice.

2 The mice on the sleeve creep round it by using one mouse from each line in turn as a motif. They are staggered by half a position so that they overlap by this amount on the knitting. Reverse the positions for the other sleeve so that the mice are coming round both sleeves the same way.

3 Begin the motifs about 20 rows above the welt. Place the first mouse on the 24 needles to the left of centre o (to right on second sleeve).

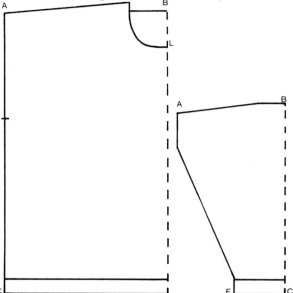

63 Diagrams for the mouse and cat jumpers

Ladies' mice

Body	AB =	21.5	22	24	25	26.5	28	cm
		$8\frac{1}{2}$	$8\frac{3}{4}$	$9\frac{1}{2}$	$9\frac{3}{4}$	$10\frac{1}{2}$	11	in.
	BL =	7						cm
		$2\frac{3}{4}$						in.
	AC =	53	56	59	61	64	64	cm
		$20\frac{3}{4}$	22	$23\frac{3}{4}$	24	$25\frac{1}{4}$	$25\frac{1}{4}$	in.
Sleeve	EC =	10	11	11.5	11.5	12	12.5	cm
		4	$4\frac{1}{4}$	$4\frac{1}{2}$	$4\frac{1}{2}$	$4\frac{3}{4}$	5	in.
	AB =	18	19	20	20.5	22	23	cm
		7	$7\frac{1}{2}$	8	$8\frac{1}{2}$	$8\frac{3}{4}$	9	in.
	BC =	43	45	46	46	47	47	cm
		17	$17\frac{3}{4}$	18	18	$18\frac{1}{2}$	$18\frac{1}{2}$	in.

Children's cats

Body	AB =	15	16	17.5	18	19.5	cm
		6	$6\frac{1}{4}$	$6\frac{3}{4}$	7	$7\frac{3}{4}$	in.
	AC =	38	42	46	47.5	50	cm
		15	$16\frac{1}{2}$	18	$18\frac{3}{4}$	$19\frac{3}{4}$	in.
Sleeve	EC =	9	10	11	12	13.5	cm
		$3\frac{1}{2}$	4	$4\frac{1}{4}$	$4\frac{3}{4}$	$5\frac{1}{4}$	in.
	AB =	13	15	16	17	18	cm
		5	6	$6\frac{1}{4}$	$6\frac{3}{4}$	7	in.
	BC =	28	30	30	31.5	34	cm
		11	$11\frac{3}{4}$	$11\frac{3}{4}$	$12\frac{1}{2}$	$13\frac{1}{2}$	in.

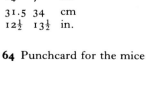

64 Punchcard for the mice

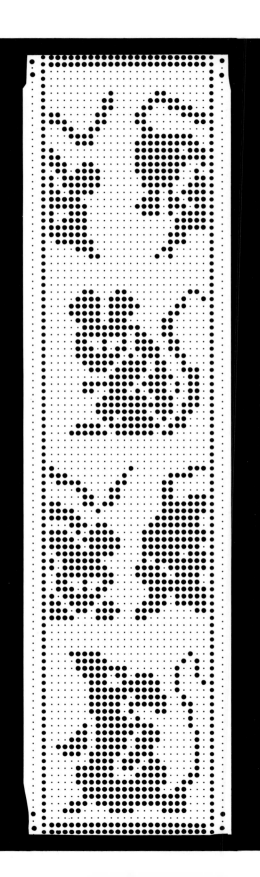

FRONT

Push forward to WP 151 161 169 177 187 195 needles.

Push every 3rd needle to NWP and using WY cast on over remainder. Knit a few rows. Change to MT − 3.

Knit 2 rows in fine thread.

Change to MY and knit 28 rows, all sizes.

Knit 1 loose row. Knit 30 rows MT − 2.

Fill empty needles and pick up hem from first row in fine thread.

RC 000.

Change to MT, engage punchcard and lock on row 1.

Knit 1 row.

Release card and continue in pattern throughout.

Knit to RC 115 130 140 142 154 154.

Mark each end with coloured yarn for armhole.

Knit to RC 184 206 222 230 236 236.

Mark st number 10 11 12 14 16 16 each side of centre. Knit 12 rows.

* Mark st number 22 23 25 28 30 30 each side of centre.

Knit to RC 226 236 240 260 275 275.

Mark neck sts as at *.

Shape shoulders

Push 10 sts to HP at both ends of next 8 rows.

Knit 1 row across all needles.

Release centre neck sts from machine (no need to hold on WY as they are going to be cut out).

Take shoulders off onto WY, or cast off round sinker pins.

BACK

Cast on and knit as front to RC 226 236 240 260 275 275.

Mark st number 22 23 25 28 30 30 each side of centre 0.

Shape shoulders and finish as front.

SLEEVES

Push forward to WP 71 79 81 81 85 89 needles.

Push every 3rd needle to NWP and cast on with WY over remainder.

Make hem as front.

RC 000.

Change to MT − 1 for st st.

Inc 1 st at beg of next 2 rows and every 4th and 5th rows to 129 135 145 147 155 163 sts.

Knit to RC 170 176 180 180 186 186.

Set carr to hold.

On next 4 rows push 20 sts opposite carr to HP, wrapping inside needles. Knit 1 row over all sts.

Take off onto WY or cast off loosely.

Stitch with sewing machine just outside markers on back and front. Cut out neck. Join both shoulders by sewing or grafting.

NECKBAND

Using WY cast on 150 150 156 160 160 166 sts (approx).

Change to MY and MT.

Knit 6 rows st st.

Transfer every 3rd st for mock rib.

Knit 12 rows, gradually dec tension to MT − 4.

Knit 1 loose row.

Knit 12 rows, gradually inc tension to MT.

Bring empty needles to WP and knit 6 rows st st.

Take off onto WY.

TO MAKE UP

Pin the neckband to the garment with cast-on edge to the outside and stocking stitch rows covering the cut edge. Unravelling the waste yarn a few stitches at a time, back-stitch into place. Fold the neckband over to the inside, to cover the cut edge, and stitch down. The row of holes made by bringing empty needles to working position is on the inside of the neck.

Sew in sleeves and join side and sleeve seams.

Children's cat jumper in 4-ply

| *To fit* | 56 | 61 | 66 | 71 | 76 | cm |
| | 22 | 24 | 26 | 28 | 30 | in. |

Materials Main colour 130–200gm 4-ply acrylic or Courtelle/nylon. 50gm contrast colour

Tension 31 sts and 36 rows to 10cm (4 in.) at MT approx 9 measured over Fair Isle

PATTERN NOTES

1 The shoulders are not sloped. The seams are short for children and can be cast off straight.

2 For the three smaller sizes make an opening on the shoulder. Leave a few stitches on waste yarn nearest to the neck edge. These can be picked up

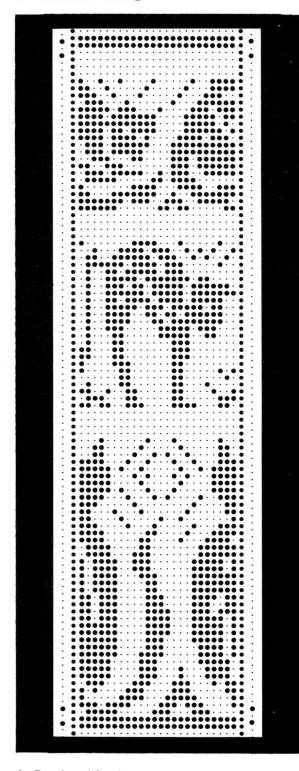

65 Punchcard for the cats

in one piece from back and front together and a narrow band knitted on with two or three button-holes made on one side. The band will fold over at the shoulder end and can be stitched to hold it in place.

3 Make sure you cut out the neck large enough. A wider band can always be knitted if it seems big.

FRONT
Push forward to WP 92 98 104 114 120 needles.
Push every 3rd needle back to NWP and using WY cast on over remainder. Knit a few rows.
Change to MT − 3.
Knit 2 rows in fine thread.
Change to MY and knit 18 rows, all sizes.
Knit 1 loose row.
At MT − 2 knit 20 rows.
Fill empty needles and pick up first row of hem in fine thread to make hem.
RC 000.
Change to MT, engage punchcard and lock on row 1.
Knit 1 row, release card, insert second colour, set for Fair Isle and knit in pattern throughout.
Knit to RC 78 84 93 98 113.
Mark edge sts for armhole.
Knit to RC 110 116 124 130 140.
Mark 7 8 8 10 10 sts each side of centre 0.
Knit 10 rows. Mark 15 16 17 18 20 sts each side of centre 0.
Knit to RC 130 136 148 152 168.
Release centre neck sts from machine, and take shoulders off onto WY, or cast off round sinker pins.

BACK
Knit as front to RC 130 136 148 152 168.
Release centre 30 32 34 36 40 sts from machine.
Take off shoulders as front.

SLEEVES
Push forward to WP 50 54 58 64 70 needles.
Push every 3rd needle to NWP for mock rib.
Cast on with WY. Knit a few rows.
Change to MY and to MT − 3 and make hem as front.
Change to MT − 1 for st st.
Inc 1 st at beg of next 2 rows and every 5th and 6th row to 80 90 96 104 112 sts.

Knit to RC 84 94 112 126 135.

On next 4 rows push 15 needles opposite carr to HP.

Knit 1 row over all sts. Take off onto WY or cast off round sinker pins.

Join one shoulder seam.

NECKBAND

Using WY cast on 80 86 89 94 102 sts. Knit a few rows.

Change to MY and MT.

Knit 4 rows.

Transfer every 3rd st for mock rib.

MT − 2. Knit 10 rows, gradually dec tension to MT − 4.

Knit 1 loose row.

Knit 10 rows, gradually inc tension to MT − 1.

Taking empty needles to WP, knit 4 rows and take off on WY.

TO MAKE UP

Attach the neckband as on the mouse jumper. Join the other shoulder seam, leaving an opening on the three smallest sizes. Sew in the sleeves and join side and sleeve seams.

Men's Fair Isle jumper with saddle shoulders

To fit   91   96   101   106   cm
            36   38   40   42   in.

Materials   Shetland wool 2/8 500gm total: colour A (used for pattern and welts) 200gm; colour B, colour C, colour D 100gm each

Tension   36 sts and 32 rows to 10cm (4 in.) at MT approx 9.1 measured over Fair Isle on washed swatch

66 Diagram of the men's Fair Isle jumper with saddle shoulders, knitted in Shetland wool

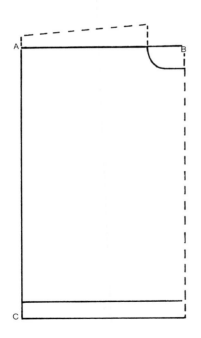
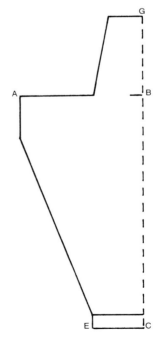

Body   AB = 24   25   26   28   cm
                9½   9¾   10¼   11   in.
          AC = 67   67   69   69   cm
                26½   26½   27¼   27¼   in.

Sleeve   AB = 24   25   25   25   cm
                  9½   9¾   9¾   9¾   in.
            EC = 11   11.5   12   12   cm
                  4¼   4½   4¾   4¾   in.
            GC = 60   61   62   62   cm
                  23½   24   24½   24½   in.

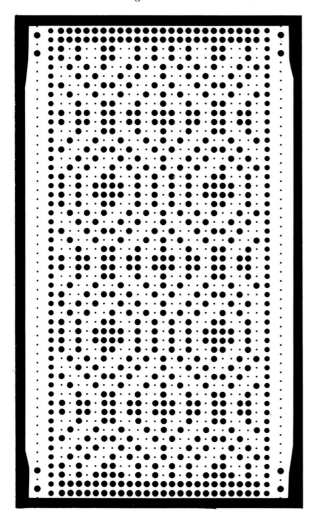

67 Punchcard for all-over Fair Isle design

PATTERN NOTES

1 106cm (42 in.) is the largest size that can be made on the machine at this tension. If you knit this pattern in an acrylic yarn, giving a tension of fewer stitches to 10cm (4 in.), then a much larger size is possible.

2 If knitting the jumper in two colours only, or if using a single bed colour change to stripe the background, the card should be punched out exactly as shown in fig. 67, or one repeat made on the electronic sheet. If you are striping the background and using the knitting carriage then the card must be punched in reverse so that the colours can be changed in the front feeder.

With single bed colour changes, yarn colours are changed in the back feeder. The pattern will knit in colour A in the front feeder. Colours must be changed at the left – if necessary knit an extra row at the beginning. Hang a claw weight at the left of the work, moving it up every few rows to prevent the changing yarns from pulling up the edge.

3 The shoulder section is added onto the sleeve, so fewer rows are knitted on the back and front. A garment without the saddle shoulder would require about 20 rows, more length.

4 *Stripe pattern for the background colours* The sequence is 6 4 2 4 rows in different colours, repeated. Thus: 6 rows colour B, 4 rows colour C, 2 rows colour D, 4 rows colour B, 6 rows colour C, 4 rows colour D, and so on. Each colour knits a different number of rows for three repeats of the sequence, although they are used in the same order throughout. It gives a varied and random look to the stripes.

BACK

Push forward 170 180 188 196 needles to WP.
Push every 3rd needle to NWP for mock rib.
Using WY cast on and knit a few rows.
Change to MY and MT − 3.
Knit 26 rows, then 1 loose row. Change to MT − 2 and knit 26 rows.
Make hem, or fill empty needles.
Insert punchcard and lock on row 1.
RC 000.
Change to MT.
Knit 1 row to select pattern needles.
Release card, insert colour 3 as background colour, into front feeder on knitting carr, or into back feeder with colour changer (see note 2).
Continue in stripe sequence to RC 110 110 120 120.
Mark edge sts for armhole.
Knit to RC 190 190 200 200.
Mark st number 36 each side of centre 0.
Take off onto WY.

FRONT

Cast on and knit as back to RC 160 160 170 170.
Mark sts for neck, 10th st each side of centre 0.
Knit 10 rows and mark 20th st each side of 0.
Knit to RC 190 190 200 200.

Mark 36th st each side of o.
Take off onto WY.

SLEEVES

Push forward 80 84 86 88 needles to WP.
Push every 3rd needle to NWP. Cast on and make hem as on back.
RC 000.
Change to MT. Insert punchcard and lock on row 1.
Knit 1 row to select pattern needles. Release card.
Knit in pattern as on back, inc 1 st at beg of every 2nd and 3rd row to 170 180 180 184 sts.
Continue to knit to RC 146 150 156 156.
Leaving centre 36 sts, take off those at each side onto WY, or cast off round sinker pins.
RC 000.
Continue to knit in pattern on remaining sts, dec 1st at both ends of next and every 10th row to RC 56 60 64 64.
Cast off.

NECKBAND

Using WY cast on 170 sts.
Change to MY and MT. Knit 1 row.
Transfer every 3rd st to next needle for mock rib.
RC 000.
Knit 14 rows, gradually dec tension to MT − 3.
Knit 1 loose row.
Knit 14 rows, gradually inc tension to MT. Bring all empty needles to WP. Knit 6 rows across all needles and release onto WY.

TO MAKE UP

Cut and sew the neckline, using the marked stitches at the front as a guide. Using the grafting/mattress-stitch technique, sew in the sleeves and saddle shoulders.

Pin the neckband in place round neckline with the cast-on side to the outside. The holes made by pulling the empty needles to working position will then be inside the neck. See that the cut edge of the neck is covered by the stocking stitch rows and does not show through the mock rib.

Unravelling the waste yarn a little at a time, back-stitch the neckband into place.

Sew side and sleeve seams.

Tack a thread through the mock rib hems and pull them together slightly before washing the garment. Remove the thread after pressing.

Variations

One punchcard can produce several different patterns. For example, try using the card for the slip-stitch zip jacket in chapter 9 for a Fair Isle pattern. If you lock a card on one row and continue to knit in Fair Isle then you will get a striped fabric with stripes of different widths. If you allow the card to revolve for a few rows and then lock again it will give yet another selection of needles for the stripes. Elongating the card so that it only revolves on alternate rows can also give variety to the designs. Try repeats at normal length alternated with double-length patterns.

When you have designed a punchcard with some particular article in mind, always play with it and see if it will provide other interesting patterns. Try changing colours for a Fair Isle pattern. Perhaps the same card would give an interesting tuck fabric, or if elongated and knitted in slip stitch it would produce an unexpected textured appearance. Most tuck and slip designs are completely altered by changing the colours of the yarns every two or four rows, giving a geometric pattern on the knit side of the work, sometimes also producing a ridged effect.

CHAPTER 8

More than two colours

Knitting more than two colours in a row can be done in four ways:

1 By hand selection of the third (or more) colours.

2 By using the slip setting on a specially punched card.

3 By the intarsia method of knitting.

4 By using holding position.

Hand selection

This method is usually used where only a small area of colour is wanted, or is combined with a punchcard. Bring the needles forward and lay the yarn across in front of the latch, then push them back to knit the stitch. The extra colours can be left on the floor at the front of the machine. The needles knitted are brought forward to holding position and the carriage set to hold – the rest of the row can then be knitted with a punchcard, or with the background colour.

The first example (fig. 68) is a simple shape made by selecting needles for the diamond while knitting an overall pattern on alternating needles. Secure the sides as for any single motif.

Try to make the hand-knitted stitches the same size as the rest. The usual fault is to make them too small by not pushing the needle back far enough.

Take care not to catch the floats from the previous row as you knit the holding position stitches. Push all the needles back so that the latches are resting on the floats and they cannot slip underneath them. Then it is quick to knit the stitches by hand.

When returning needles from holding position to be selected by the punchcard, place them into working position or upper working position as the pattern requires.

On the second example (fig. 69) the needles to be knitted by hand are actually punched onto the card. This is the simple shape of the tree trunk. The card is designed in such a way that the top of the tree is not knitted until the house roof is finished. The house and background are knitted with the Fair Isle setting in two colours. The branches of the tree are then knitted in Fair Isle, and the last two rows of the house and the chimney are selected by hand. Make sure you will recognize which needles they are and which row they are to be knitted on. They will be five or seven rows down inside the machine at the point where they are to be knitted. It is easier to see what is happening to the pattern on a machine that preselects the punched needles, but for all machines, mark where the pattern changes are on the side of the card.

This design is knitted as two single motifs and needs to have all the edges secured, but having so many extra yarns can be confusing, so wrap only the outer edges of the house and tree trunk, and when the work is finished stitch along the opposite edges, just catching the stitches together.

Using the slip setting

Only those needles selected by the holes in the punchcard (or marks on the electronic sheet) will knit. It is therefore theoretically possible to knit up to 24 colours in a row by punching out a card which will only select a needle for one colour at a

68 Hand-selecting a third colour in the middle of a two-colour design. Return needles to the position where they will knit in the correct colour

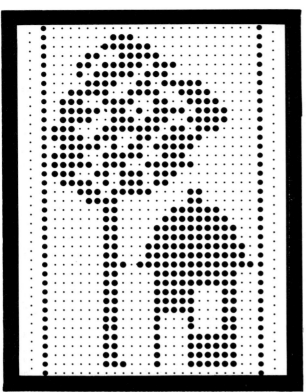

69 Knitting a third colour in the row from the punchcard. The tree trunk is knitted by hand until the roof ends, then the tree is knitted by the punchcard and the chimney is hand-selected

70 The complete tree and house motif

time. In fact it is not practicable to use more than four, because the floats on the reverse will build up to make the fabric very stiff and thick.

Two rows are knitted in each colour in order to bring the carriage back to the same side of the machine every time to change the colours. This is made quicker by using a colour changer. Increase the tension to avoid a narrowing of the knitting.

This technique is illustrated by the punchcard in fig. 71 which will produce three colours of stripes repeated across the fabric.

Set the carriage to slip and knit two rows in colour A, two rows in colour B and two rows in colour C. Although you have made six passes of the carriage across the machine, only two complete rows have been knitted.

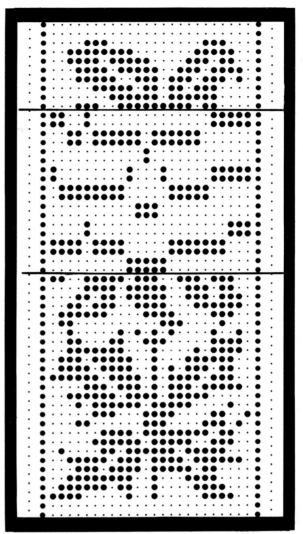

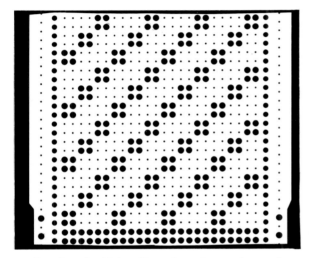

71 Punchcard which will produce three colours of stripes in one row, by setting the machine to slip. Change colours every two movements of the carriage

Anemone

This flower (fig. 72) is knitted using the Fair Isle setting with two colours threaded up, and changing to slip setting for the six rows knitted in three colours in the centre of the flower. The third colour can be fed in by holding it firmly in your hand above the carriage.

When marking out a card to knit part of a Fair Isle pattern in a third colour, remember that the background colour, as well as the design, must be punched out or it will not knit.

72 Anemone design. Knit as normal Fair Isle until the first line is reached, change to slip and knit two rows with each colour for 18 movements of the carriage, giving six complete rows. Return to Fair Isle and two-colour knitting to finish the design
Yarn used for the slip section: centre of the flower = A, flower petals = B, background colour = C
Knit two rows A, two rows B, 2 rows C. Repeat twice more

Long floats will occur in the slip stitch section. As these are only over six rows, they are easily dealt with by hooking them up, or a strip of iron-on interfacing could be attached behind the area. Supershape Vilene has some sideways stretch. This method could be used to introduce small areas of a third or fourth colour to many designs:

black and white patches on a cat, apples on a tree, or the centres of diamond shapes knitted in different colours for each repeat of the card.

Intarsia knitting

Blocks of colour are knitted using a separate ball of yarn for each one, so that no floats are carried across the back of the knitting. This enables you to knit as many colours on one row as you wish. It is useful for incorporating complicated coloured patterns into the work in any position. There is no restriction of 24-stitch repeats.

Some models of machine can knit intarsia using their normal carriage (see your instruction book for this). It is very difficult to see the positions to change yarns and it is very much easier to use the separate intarsia carriages which are now produced for all models. The carriage is taken across the machine empty. This brings all needles forward to upper working position (the stitches will *not* drop off). The separate colours are laid across the needles by hand before taking the carriage across to knit the stitches.

Prepare the number of coloured yarns you will use by winding them into small balls round a piece of card. Make a slit in the side of the card to anchor the end of yarn so that it hangs below the machine and will not unravel. There needs to be a little tension on the yarn as it is laid across the needles and the hanging balls will provide this. If they are very small, only sufficient for a few stitches, add extra weight by clipping a spring clothespeg onto them. There is an intarsia yarn brake made by Tricot which hangs in front of the machine and will provide tension for up to 16 separate yarns, also stopping them from tangling. Full instructions for use are provided with this.

On the first row hold the end of each yarn until it is safely anchored in the stitches. On the second, and on all subsequent rows, begin with the thread nearest to the carriage and take that across the needles according to the chart. Bring the second yarn up underneath the first and lay that across the next set of needles. The two yarns have crossed over one another below the needles (fig. 73). Repeat this across the row with every yarn. If the yarns do not loop round one another where the colours change you will be knitting unconnected blocks of colour which will have slits up each side.

A separate length of yarn must be used for every section of colour, even if it is only one stitch wide. For example, an animal with four legs standing next to a flower will require four balls of 'leg' colour, one ball for the stem of the flower, and six balls of background colour. If a single stitch has the same colour on each side of it, in practice it is easier to carry the colour across the needle instead of having two balls. By studying the chart of the design first it is possible to work out the numbers of yarn balls needed.

Using a charter makes intarsia knitting easier because the pattern can be drawn onto the sheet in the position it is required and as the sheet revolves each change of colour can be seen row by row. If you do not have a charter, draw the design onto squared paper, and colour each area in clearly. Mark the paper with rows and stitches so that you can see where you are on the sheet at a glance by looking at the row counter and using the needle numbers appropriate to where the pattern is to be placed on the garment.

The tension may be different when knitted with the intarsia carriage from that knitted by the normal carriage – even when set to the same tension number – so it is advisable to knit the whole of the garment piece with the design on it with the intarsia carriage, even if there are quite large sections knitted in one colour. If the garment has plain sleeves and back they should also be knitted using the intarsia carriage, but since it is much slower to work like this – and also as the tension may not be quite so even over large plain areas when laying the yarn across by hand – it is more practicable to knit these pieces with the normal knitting carriage. As always, check the tension first in case any minor adjustments need to be made.

The chart design in fig. 74 could be knitted onto a jumper based on the basic pattern.

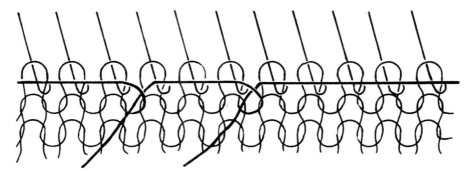

73 The yarns must cross over one another below the needles when knitting intarsia patterns

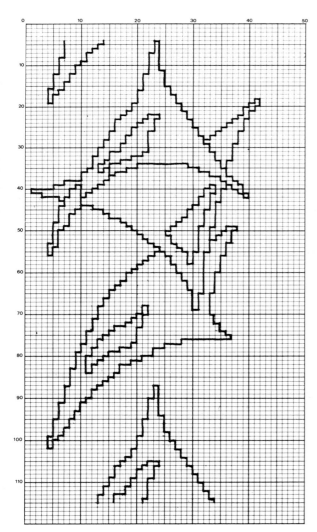

74 Chart for an intarsia design. This can be used up just one side of a garment and repeated for the length required

Using holding position

A pattern with no floats can be knitted by using the holding position so that only one block of needles at a time is in use. Not such intricate designs can be knitted as when using the intarsia carriage, but different colours can be used for each section, and different stitch patterns as well.

Set carriage to hold. Bring needles to holding position to make the slanting pattern as required. Wrap the inside needles in holding position to avoid holes. After knitting one section, the needles needed for the second colour are taken to upper working position where they will knit back to working position on the next row. You must fill in the area which was in hold first. Otherwise the knitting will end up longer at one side than the other. The row counter must be turned back to the row on which each previous section began. Otherwise you will lose track of the number of rows knitted. In the sample shown in fig. 76 the row counter could be on number 58 if it had not been reset but in fact only 22 rows have been knitted.

To knit a punchcard motif when some needles are in holding position, make sure that the whole motif will fit onto the area of one background colour. It becomes complicated to restart the punchcard pattern if needles are to be put to holding position in the middle of it. Either stick to a one-colour background or change the background colour in a horizontal straight line across the whole motif.

The second colour, in feeder two, must be removed after knitting the motif as the carriage approaches the needles in HP, or it will catch on

75 A picture may be made by partially knitting the rows in different colours

the last needle in holding position and make a long loop. Replace it in the feeder before the carriage reaches the motif needles.

By looking at the sample in fig. 75 it can be seen how, by superimposing one or two punchcard designs onto the pattern of 'fields and mountains', a picture could be knitted. The house and tree design (fig. 69) added at the bottom and a bird in the sky would complete it.

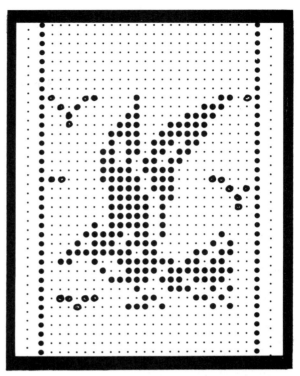

77 Punchcard for a bird. If using this as a repeating motif, add extra 'birds' as shown by the circles to avoid very long floats between the motifs

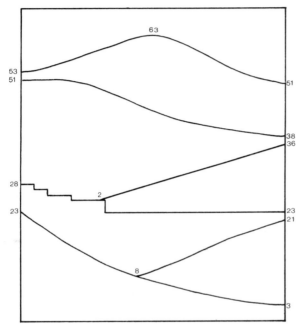

76 The row counter must be returned to the number at the beginning of each holding position section before knitting the next area

CHAPTER 9

Textured knitting

Cables

Cable stitches originated on the fisherman's jersey. They were an attempt to copy the pattern of the ropes which played an important part in his life. They were not only equipment for the boat, but also a symbol of life itself – the 'lifelines' to which he could cling, or throw overboard to a drowning man. Each village and, in places, each family, developed its own designs, so that you could tell where the man came from by the pattern of his jersey.

The cable is made by removing two adjacent groups of two or three stitches from the machine onto transfer tools, crossing them over one another and placing each set on the opposite needles.

Although making cables is a hand technique, it is worth the extra trouble involved because it always looks neat and a classic cabled jumper never looks dated. It is a way of making a plain garment more interesting without being too complicated, but it does take time, and some concentration so that you don't lose your place.

Use a strong yarn for cable patterns. A soft Shetland wool will break more easily than a mixture or acrylic yarn. The stitches are put under considerable strain when they are twisted over one another and repairs are difficult if the yarn snaps in mid-twist.

There are two methods which give more stretch to the stitches which are to be transferred.

1 Place the stitches each side of the cables in non-working position. Before beginning on the pattern, transfer the stitches to the next needle and leave these needles out of work.

2 Remove the stitches each side of the cables onto spare yarn, but leave the needles in working position to knit normally. When the row where the cable twist is to be made is reached, drop these side stitches off the needles and allow them to ladder down, keeping the needle in working position. This gives even more space for stretching the stitches across. When the cables are finished, if you wish, this loose row of threads can be latched up to give a line of purl stitches (knit stitches as the knitting faces you on the machine) alongside the cable. This can be done quite quickly before removing the work from the machine.

These methods also show off the cable more by making it stand out from the background. Do not use fluffy or tweed mixture yarns. A plain colour and a smooth yarn will give the best definition.

A cable can be added to any plain jumper pattern. The twists do tend to tighten up the knitting, but this tightening is compensated for somewhat by the stitches left out of work alongside the cables. Two or three lines of cables will make very little difference. It is only if the whole piece is cabled that it will be significantly narrowed.

When making several cables across a garment, the twists should be staggered so that they are made on different rows. It could become impossible to twist stitches over one another if they are all on the same row. As it is, the stitches are tight, and to make sure they will knit off on the next row, bring all cable needles forward to D or E position and set the carriage to knit them back.

Try to arrange the cable twists to come at regular intervals, say every five or ten rows. For

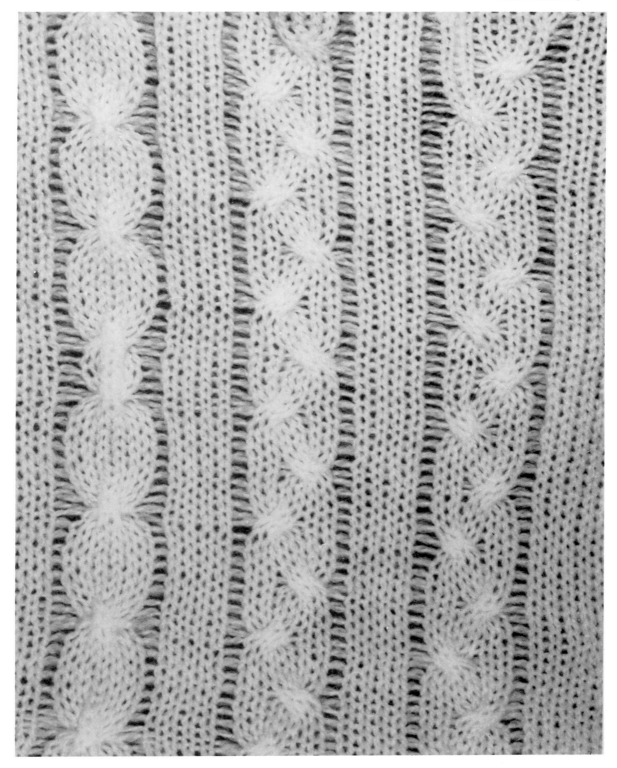

78 Cable patterns. *Left* Chain cable   *Centre* Double twist   *Right* Double twist reversed

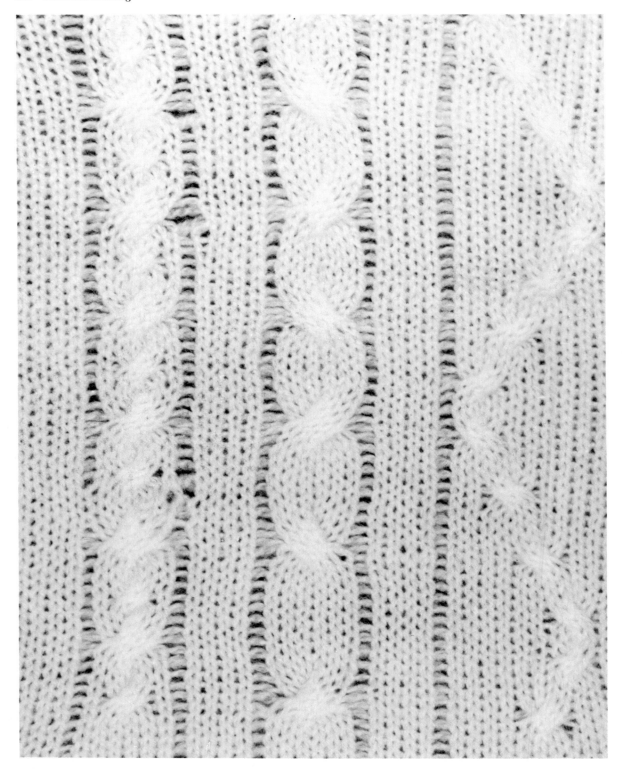

79 Cable patterns. *Left* Cable within a cable   *Centre* Wavy line   *Right* Travelling twists

example, if you are making three cables across a garment, make the centre twist at row 5, the two outside ones at row 10, centre at row 15, and so one. You will then know just where you are, by looking at the row counter. If the intervals cannot be made as simple as this, make a checklist of the rows for each cable before you start, in case of interruptions.

True cables should always twist over one another in the same direction. If the first twist is made to the left and the second to the right, a wavy line will result. This may produce an interesting pattern, but it is not a cable.

A little jingle like 'right in, left out' makes it easier to remember which way to cross each time (right-hand stitches transferred towards the centre of the knitting, and left-hand ones towards the outside edge).

When the first set of stitches is removed from the needles, hang the transfer tool on the adjacent needles while you remove and transfer the second set, then the stitches will not slip off while you are manipulating the others.

Machine-knitted cables are made with two or three stitches twisted round one another at regular intervals. This is the widest that can be twisted easily, three stitches over three. Too much strain is put on the needles to make a wider cable in this way. There are many variations, and many different cable patterns. Different numbers of rows between the twists can change the appearance of the pattern. For example, make two twists close together, then have a gap of 20 rows and repeat – these twists can be alternated in parallel columns.

You will probably think of some new ideas yourself but here are a few different styles.

1 *Chain cable* The centre twist looks like the edge of a chain link. Use seven needles, and drop the stitch at each side to make more 'give'. Cross stitch numbers 1 and 2 with 6 and 7, leaving the centre two stitches in place. Knit ten rows and repeat. This can be varied by leaving only one stitch in the centre, crossing three over three.

2 *Double twist* Use six needles. The middle stitches are always moved outwards first. The two centre stitches are crossed with the two right-hand stitches. Knit five rows. The centre stitches are crossed with the two left-hand stitches. Knit five rows. Repeat.

3 *Double twist reversed* Use six needles. Always move outside stitches inwards first. The two right-hand stitches are placed on the centre needles, centre stitches to the right. Knit five rows. The two left-hand stitches are placed on the centre needles, centre stitches to left. Repeat.

4 *Cable within a cable* Use six needles. Make the first twist as the basic cable, cross stitches 1, 2 and 3 with stitches 4, 5 and 6. Knit five rows. Cross stitches 2 and 3 with stitches 4 and 5. Knit five rows. Repeat.

5 *Wavy line* (not really a cable, but can look decorative) Cross sets of needles (can be in twos or threes) over one another alternately to right and left. Cross stitches 1, 2 and 3 over stitches 4, 5 and 6. Knit ten rows. Cross stitches 4, 5 and 6 over 1, 2 and 3. Knit ten rows.

6 *Travelling twists* Cross stitches 1 and 2 with 3 and 4. Knit five rows. Cross 3 and 4 with 5 and 6. Knit five rows. Cross 5 and 6 with 7 and 8. Knit five rows. Continue in one direction as far as you wish, then return by reversing the crosses (cross 7 and 8 with 5 and 6 and so on). No needles are left out at sides.

7 *Two-colour cables* By knitting stripes, using the Fair Isle setting, alternate twists can be in another colour. Narrow cables are best for this as the stitches will pull tight. It is not possible to leave a needle in non-working position at each side because the floats on the back will show through. Punch out one line on a card with four stitches to knit at intervals in a second colour, and lock on this row. Make the twists over four stitches in the colour A column alternated with twists in the colour B column.

8 *Two-colour variations* A card punched out as shown in fig. 80 and knitted in Fair Isle will produce two-colour cables if the stitches are twisted on the last row of the second colour. Count the rows as you go and make the twists every six rows. The punchcard can be varied so that the stripes are more widely spaced, or are three stitches wide instead of two.

9 *Corded cable* Knit the basic cable of three stitches crossed with the adjacent three. When the knitting is complete, make a cord and thread it through the cable twists. Do not pull it too tightly but allow it to flow with the curves of the cable.

The cord can be in a contrast colour, or the same as the knitting. This makes a very bold pattern.

10 *Using cords sewn to the surface* Make two lengths of cord and stitch them to the surface of a plain piece of knitting, twisting them over one another at intervals to make cables. Take care to sew the cords on straight. Very small kinks in the line will spoil the effect. Do not twist the cord itself.

11 *Rope edging* Rope edging (shown as a hem finish in chapter 5) can also give a cable-like effect if it is used up the centre of the knitting instead of along the edge. Fold the knitting along one line of stitches and pick up three stitches onto the needles. Knit six rows over these stitches, then, using the three-pronged transfer tool, pick up the next three stitches and place them on the same needle. Knit six rows. Continue along the line.

Two or three rows of the rope twist made close together is very effective, and can also be used on the purl side of the knitting.

12 *Chunky cable* A wider, more chunky cable can be made by knitting extra rows on one or both of the crossover sections. Up to about ten stitches can be used, crossing five over five. However, this means that you will need two multiple-transfer tools. If you have only one, then the second set of stitches can, with great care, be held on two transfer tools of three and two prongs.

Isolate the cable section by placing all the stitches each side of it into holding position. Knit ten rows on half the cable stitches, place them into holding position and work ten rows on the five remaining stitches. Cross the stitches over one another, move the five stitches in holding position from their needles and place the second group of five onto them, then cross the first set behind the second.

Extra rows can be knitted on one half of the cable stitches. All the others should be in holding position. Knit ten rows on five stitches. Place these needles in holding position, and knit five rows on all others.

The stitches with the ten rows will roll into a tube and appear thinner than the other five stitches, and these should be the ones crossing on the knit side of the fabric.

Take five stitches off the needles, cross the ten-row strip across to these five needles. Replace the others on empty needles. This enables you to make cable crosses in different styles.

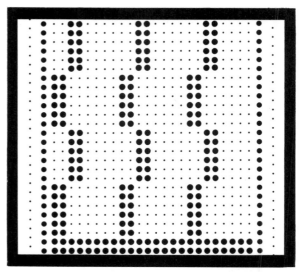

80 Punchcard for knitting two-colour cables. Make the twists every six rows

Cable jumper

To fit sizes	91	97	102	107	112	cm
	36	38	40	42	44	in.

Materials   One 500-gm cone of Atkinsons Reflections (4-ply)

Tension   34 sts and 40 rows to 10cm (4 in.) at MT approx 8

CABLE PATTERN
Seventeen blocks of 6 sts separated by a needle out of work. All cable twists begin on row 5 as follows:

Blocks 1 and 17
Chain cable, made by crossing sts 1 and 2 with 5 and 6.
Knit 10 rows between twists.

Blocks 2 and 16
Knitted in st st throughout.

Blocks 3 and 4, 15 and 16
Two columns each side of double cable. Cross sts 1 and 2 with 3 and 4, centre sts always moved first. Knit 5 rows.
Cross sts 3 and 4 with 5 and 6. Knit 5 rows.

Blocks 5 and 14
Knitted in st st throughout.

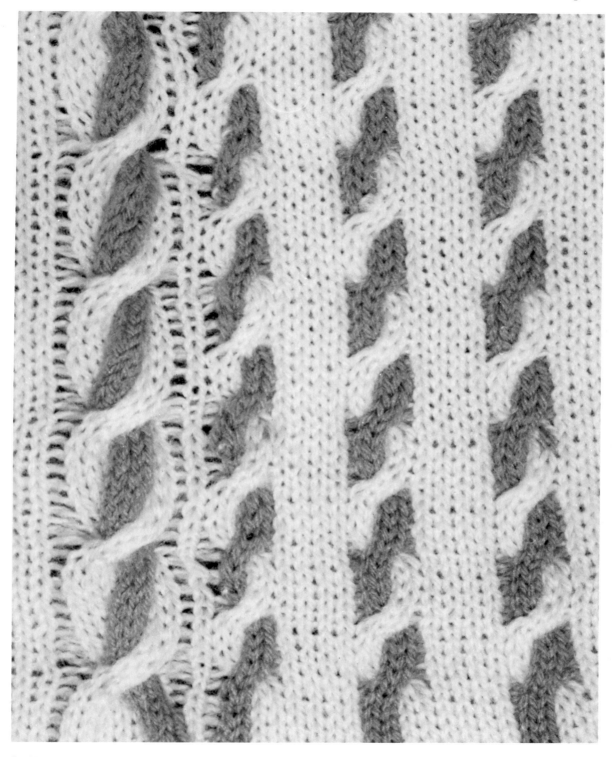

81 Two-colour cables. *Left* A cord made on second colour threaded through the basic twist   *Right* Three lengths of two-colour cables made using the punchcard

82 Cords of different thickness sewn onto the surface of the knitting

83 Diagram for the cable jumper

Body						
AB =	44	45	48	50	54	cm
	$17\frac{1}{4}$	$17\frac{3}{4}$	19	$19\frac{3}{4}$	$21\frac{1}{4}$	in.
AC =	60	62	64	66	66	cm
	$23\frac{1}{2}$	$24\frac{1}{2}$	$25\frac{1}{4}$	26	26	in.
BL =	50	52	55	57	57.5	cm
	$19\frac{3}{4}$	$20\frac{1}{2}$	$21\frac{3}{4}$	$22\frac{1}{2}$	$22\frac{3}{4}$	in.
Sleeve						
AB =	42	42	42.5	42.5	43	cm
	$16\frac{1}{2}$	$16\frac{1}{2}$	$16\frac{3}{4}$	$16\frac{3}{4}$	17	in.
BC =	41	41	43	43	44	cm
	$16\frac{1}{4}$	$16\frac{1}{4}$	17	17	$17\frac{1}{4}$	in.
EC =	22	22	22.5	22.5	23	cm
	$8\frac{3}{4}$	$8\frac{3}{4}$	$8\frac{3}{4}$	$8\frac{3}{4}$	9	in.

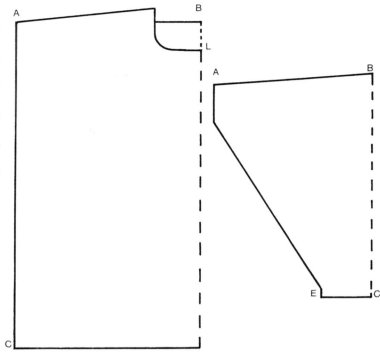

84 Diagram to show how the different twists are made in each of the 17 sections and on which rows they occur

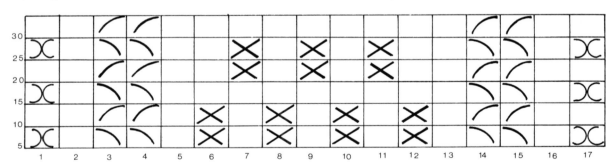

Blocks 6, 8, 10 and 12
Basic cables, cross sts 1, 2 and 3 with 4, 5 and 6. Knit 5 rows. Repeat basic cable. Knit 15 rows.

Blocks 7, 9 and 11
Knit 15 rows. Beg these cables 10 rows after those on 6, 8, 10 and 12 have been done. Basic cable, cross 1, 2 and 3 with 4, 5 and 6. Knit 5 rows. Repeat basic cable. Knit 15 rows.

Figure 84 shows which cables are worked on each row. After the first repeat you will be able to see which ones are to be crossed next from the knitting. Take care to cross the double cables in opposite directions each time. The pattern of the zig-zag twists can be seen on the purl side facing you.

BACK
Cast on with WY 149 155 165 173 183 sts.
Knit a few rows and transfer every 3rd st to next needle for a mock rib.
Change to MY and MT–3.
Knit 20 rows.
Knit 1 loose fold row.
Change to MT–2.
Knit 20 rows.

Fill all empty needles or pick up hem.
RC 000.
Knit 1 row over all needles at MT.
Counting from centre 0, transfer 4th and every following 7th st to next needle number 60, on each side of bed. Push these needles to NWP. Knit 4 rows.
RC 5.
Begin pattern by crossing sts for the cables as described above.
Knit to RC 140 145 145 145 150.
Commence small edge rib: 3 sts in, cross 2 sts over 2 every 5 rows to make a narrow cable each side to edge the dropped shoulder.
Knit to RC 237 242 253 260 266.
Take centre 59 61 63 65 65 sts off onto WY.

Shape shoulders
Knit 1 row over left shoulder needles. Keeping cable pattern correct, push 15 15 20 20 20 sts to HP at shoulder edge on next 2 rows. Knit 1 row over all needles.
RC 243 248 259 266 272.
Take off on WY, or cast off loosely behind sinker pins.
Complete right shoulder to match.

FRONT
Cast on and knit as for the back to RC 207 211 222 228 231.

Shape neck
COL.
Fill empty needles over the centre (29 31 31 33 35 sts) and push them to HP together with needles at right-hand side.
Continuing on sts at left, on next 8 rows push 1 needle to HP at neck edge.
Knit 10 rows.

Shape shoulders as for back and take off onto WY, or cast off. Complete right side to match.
Do not remove stitches in HP from machine.

NECKBAND
Pick up 10 sts each side of front neck onto next needles.
Replace back neck sts onto machine alongside the front, leaving 5 needles empty between them.
Pick up 5 sts from side of back neck onto these and 5 needles at other side (total of approx 134 138 140 144 144 sts).

RC 000.
Knit 1 row MT over all sts.
Starting at left edge, transfer 3rd and 8th sts alternately to next needle across the bed. Push needles to NWP, leaving alt groups of 2 and 4 sts.
MT−1. Knit 2 rows.
On every group of 4 needles, cross first 2 sts over the second two. Knit 4 rows. Repeat cables. Reduce tension by 2 dots every 4 rows and make 2 more sets of cables, 4 in all. Reduce tension by 2 more dots and knit 4 rows.
RC 24.
Knit 1 loose fold row. Gradually inc tension to MT−1, knit 24 rows without any further cables.
RC 49.
Take off onto WY.

SLEEVES
Cast on with WY 75 75 77 77 81 sts.
Make hem as back, and fill empty needles.
RC 000.
MT. Knit 1 row, inc 1 st both ends.
Beg at centre, transfer 4th, 10th and 17th sts each side to next needle. Push needles to NWP (5 blocks of 6 sts).
Knit 4 rows.

Cable pattern (alternating cables as centre of back and front)
Make basic cable over blocks 1, 3 and 5. Knit 5 rows. Repeat cables. Knit 10 rows. Make basic cables over blocks 2 and 4. Knit 5 rows. Repeat cables.
Inc 1 st at both ends of every 3rd row to RC 19.
After this inc at both ends of every 5th row to 143 143 145 145 147 sts.
Knit 25 25 30 30 30 rows straight.
RC 165 165 175 177 183.
Shape top of sleeve by putting 10 needles to HP at each side opposite carr over next 6 rows. Knit across all needles and take off onto WY or cast off round sinker pins.

TO MAKE UP
Graft or sew shoulders together. Turn in neckband and sew down through open stitches. Sew sleeves into place level with the small edge cable. Turn up hems and cuffs if they were not completed on the machine and sew side and sleeve seams.

85 The neckband with the small cables, and the alternating pairs of twists on the centre front, flanked by double cables

Slip stitch

Slip stitch is an often very neglected stitch pattern, usually because there is not such a pronounced textured effect as when using the more popular tuck stitch. When the machine is set for slip, or skip, only the needles selected by the holes on the punchcard, or the marks on the electronic sheet, will be brought to upper working position and knitted normally. All others will remain in working position and the yarn will pass in front of these stitches. This makes floats across the fabric rather like those made when knitting Fair Isle, so the fabric is pulled in to make a firm material. The floats themselves make the pattern on the purl surface of the knitting.

Chapter 5 describes how slip stitch can be used for making a less bulky waistband and the same pattern, selecting alternate needles for several rows (card 1 locked), can also be used to make small hems on the purl side of the fabric which looks rather like garter stitch. Knit six or eight rows slipping alternate needles, knit two rows stocking stitch and repeat several times. Try knitting each little hem in a different colour, or shades of the same colour, for a very pretty effect. This can be very decorative for collars and cuffs. One small 'hem' of slip stitch between blocks of tuck or other slip patterns accentuates the design.

If some needles are set to slip for a greater number of rows, the knitting will be pulled up by the slipped stitches to produce a ruched effect on the purl side of the garment. After knitting off the slipped stitches, if the same ones are selected again an even pattern or rows of ruched tucks is produced. By selecting different needles from the first ones a twisted ruching is produced which can be quite dramatic.

Jacket in ruched slip stitch

This garment looks best in a slightly textured yarn. Two ends of a fine industrial bouclé could be used, or one of the slubbed cottons. The yarn suggested here is a cotton-and-Shetland mixture, which is approximately a 4-ply thickness and has a soft slub texture.

To fit   86–91   96–101   cm
           34–36   38– 40   in.

Materials   550gm slub yarn, 44-cm (17-in.) zip fastener

Tension   30 stitches and 60 rows to 10cm (4 in.) at MT approx 8

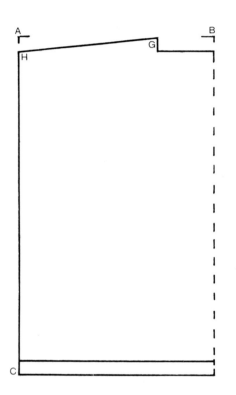

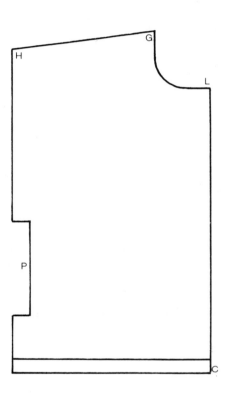

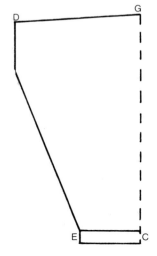

86 Slip-stitch zip-up jacket

Body   AB = 23.5 28.5 cm
                9¼   11¼   in.

         HG = 16   21   cm
                6¼   8¼   in.

         CL = 45   50   cm
                17¾   19¾   in.

         AC = 59   64   cm
                23¼   25¼   in.

         P = 13 cm (5 in.) up from bottom and 13 cm (5 in.) wide

Sleeve   EC = 11.5 cm
                  4½   in.

           CG = 46   cm
                  18   in.

           DG = 28   cm
                  11   in.

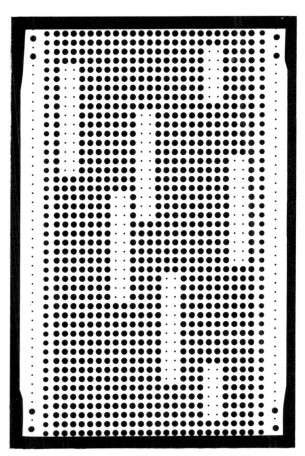

87 Punchcard for the slip pattern

Knit 1 row, release card and set carr to slip both directions.
Knit 330 360 rows.
Take centre 44 sts off onto WY.

Shape shoulder
Knit on one side only. Push 12 needles to HP at shoulder on next 2 alt rows.
Knit 1 row over all needles, take off onto WY or cast off round sinker pins.
Complete second side to match.

LEFT FRONT
Using WY cast on 70 75 sts.
Knit hem as back.
RC 000.
Change to MT. Insert punchcard and lock on row 1.
Release card and knit 80 rows in pattern.
Cast off 6 sts at side edge for pocket top recess.
Knit to RC 160.
Cast on 6 sts at side edge. Continue to knit to RC 270 300.
Cast off 12 sts at neck edge, then 1 st every alt row at neck edge until there are 48 sts. Continue straight to RC 330.
Set carr to hold and shape shoulder as back.

RIGHT FRONT
Knit as left front, reversing shapings.

SLEEVES
Cast on 70 sts with WY. Knit hem as back.
Lock on row 1. Change to MT and knit 1 row.
Release card and knit in pattern, inc 1 st at beg of every 4th and 5th rows to 170 sts. Continue to knit to RC 260. Set carr to hold and push 12 needles to HP opposite carr on next 4 rows. Knit 1 row over all needles.
Join shoulders and sew sleeves into position. Do not join side seams of body.

POCKETS
Pick up 40 sts from indented length of the side of the front, wrong (knit) side facing. Knit 16 rows at MT − 2. Knit 1 row at MT − 4. Knit 16 rows at MT − 2.
Pick up edge st from 1st row. Pick up sts below pocket top to total of 54 sts, finishing about 5cm (2 in.) above welt. Knit 100 rows at MT.

PATTERN NOTES

1 Purl side of knitting is the right side.

2 Hem is folded with the purl side out, so it cannot be picked up onto the machine needles, but must be stitched down afterwards. The fold row must be tight instead of loose.

3 Stitches at the neck edge are cast off rather than placed in holding position because they are then out of the way of the patterning needles.

BACK
Cast on with WY 140 170 sts.
Knit a few rows. Change to MT−2. Knit 20 rows.
Knit 1 row at MT−4.
Knit 20 rows at MT−2.
RC 000.
Insert punchcard (fig. 87) and lock on row 1.
Change to MT.

With wrong (knit) side of back facing, pick up sts from side of back to correspond with front. Knit 1 row and cast off loosely. Sew top and bottom of pocket bag. Stitch side of welt to front.

NECKBAND

With right (purl) side of knitting facing, pick up 42 sts from left front, 44 from back and 42 from right front.

Knit 16 rows, beg with MT and gradually reducing tension to MT − 3. Knit one tight row and knit the other side of the neckband (16 rows), gradually inc to MT.

Take off on WY and stitch down inside the neck. Finish stitching all seams, and catch pocket bag down at each corner with loose stitches.

COLOURED VARIATIONS

If the same punchcard is used and the colours changed every two or four rows, a very exciting pattern emerges on the *knit* side of the fabric. The direction of the knitting produces geometric patterns. The same design and tensions can be used.

FRONT BANDS FOR ZIP

1 Stitches can be picked up along the edge, with wrong side facing, and a band knitted which will be long enough to fold right round the tape of the zip. This will make a neat finish inside the garment, as the tape and stitching will not be seen.

For the garment knitted at the tension given, pick up approximately 80 sts along the front edge. Knit 4 rows at MT. Knit 1 tight row for the fold.

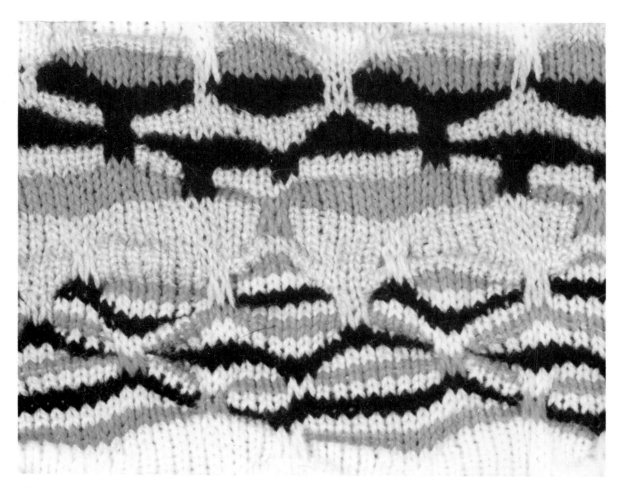

88 The same punchcard was used to change the colours every two or four rows to produce a pattern on the knit side

Knit 6 rows at MT − 1, 1 *loose* row at MT + 4, 6 rows at MT − 1 and take off on WY.

Fold the band at the tight fold row (purl side out), press lightly and tack or pin the zip into place behind the band. Fold the remaining knitting up over the tape of the zip and unravelling waste yarn a few stitches at a time, back-stitch, with matching polyester sewing thread, through the open loops and zip tape, through to the front of the garment. Band and zip are sewn in one operation.

2 A row of double crochet or crab stitch can be made along the front to give a firm edge for attaching the zip.

3 A narrow knitted band can be attached to the front, and the zip sewn behind it.

MULTICOLOURED TEXTURE

Although the use of slip stitch to produce three colours in the row is explained in chapter 7, a very interesting texture effect coupled with three coloured stripes can be achieved using the punchcard shown in fig. 89. The colour in this example is changed every six rows, and the card is designed to carry the colour for twelve rows across two other colours, so each strip of unpunched holes on the card must be twelve rows long. The second colour knits right across the row except for the needles slipping colour 1. Colour 3 has two sets of needles slipping, one holding colour 1, and the other colour 2. When colour 1 is knitted again across the row, colour 3 is held for twelve rows also.

If fewer rows were knitted in each colour then more colours could be included across the punchcard. However, it would be difficult to fit in more than four colours in the 24-stitch repeat. Try making a card which slips the colours for eight rows, changing every four rows.

It is best to stick to a simple shape for a garment made with this stitch, for example a sleeveless pullover, a waistcoat with dropped shoulders or, a jacket with very little shaping to the sleeves. The slipover in plate 12 is made from two identical pieces. Using 4-ply yarn the tension is 32 sts and 40 rows to 10cm (4 in.) at MT approx 8, and it requires approx 70 gm of each of three colours.

To fit   81   86   cm
       32   34   in.

Length   54cm (21.5 in.)

Cast on 136 sts. Make a hem and knit 396 rows then finish with another hem. Always have two stitches slipping in one of the colours at the edge. This gives a firm line of stitches to sew up the seam.

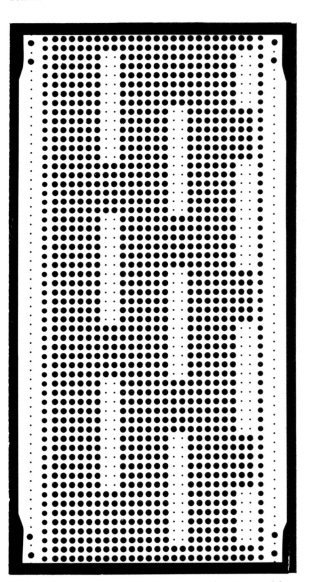

89 Punchcard used to knit the textured pattern with the three coloured stripes shown in colour plate 12

Using a variety of stitches and yarns for one design

The jacket pattern on pages 116–18 makes use of several yarns to give contrasting textures. Similar colours are suggested, all shades of beige, but you may want to include more contrast which will give a quite different appearance to the fabric.

Mixing stocking stitch, tuck and slip stitch in the same piece of knitting does present tension problems – tuck will broaden the fabric and pulls the knitting up to make it shorter by looping the threads over the needles for several rows before knitting them off. Slip stitch, on the other hand, while still shortening the knitting by pulling the stitches up, has floats across the purl side which tighten it sideways also, and the stocking stitch comes somewhere in between, widthways. You will find that the sides of the knitting are not absolutely even and for this reason it is better to stitch the garment up using a back-stitch so that the seam can be made straight. The front bands, however they are knitted, will look better if they are made to cover the edge of the knitting. They can be knitted separately and sewn onto the garment on both sides, or the stitches can be picked up on the machine. If the latter is done, make sure you compensate for the slight unevenness by picking the edge up in a straight line.

Sideways-knitted bands enable you to finish the buttonholes completely on the machine, which makes for a neat finish. Make sure they are big enough for the buttons you wish to use, as machine-made buttonholes do not have very much elasticity.

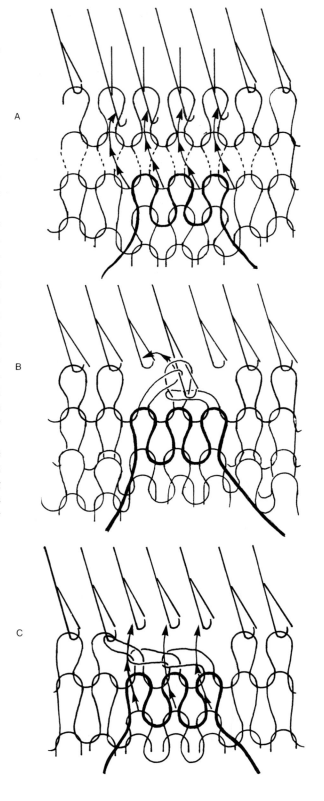

A

B

C

90 Diagram of a machine-finished buttonhole

A Stitches lifted from above the waste yarn onto the needles
B Each stitch knitted through then moved back to left-hand needle
C Stitches picked up from below the waste yarn to complete

To work machine-finished buttonholes

Knit one-quarter of the rows of the band.

Using a length of yarn in a contrasting colour, knit the stitches required for the buttonhole (e.g. four stitches) by hand.

Knit to halfway through the band. Knit the fold row. Knit three-quarters of the band.

Pick up the stitches from *above* the row of waste yarn onto the same needles. These are the stitches nearest to the needles when the knitting is hanging from the machine. Knit these stitches through the others so that there is only one stitch on each needle.

Place the second stitch from the right onto the right-hand needle, and knit it through. Return the stitch to the empty needle on the left.

Take the next (third) stitch from the left and place it on top of the one just moved back. Knit this through and move to the left, to the empty needle.

Repeat for as many times as necessary.

When you get to the last stitch of the buttonhole, in order for it to be cast off like the others, an extra stitch from the left must be used to put on top of the last stitch. Draw it through and move the stitch back onto the needle to the left of the buttonhole.

There are now empty needles where the buttonhole has been made. Pick up the stitches from *below* the coloured thread and place them onto the empty needles. Pull out the coloured thread and the buttonhole is complete. Knit the last quarter of the band and finish off with waste yarn or pick up the stitches from the first row and cast off.

It seems like a superfluous move to take the stitch from left to right, knit it through and move

91 Buttonhole completed on the machine

it back to the left. If you try to place the left-hand stitch onto the next needle and knit it through, as you continue along the row the stitches will become very tight indeed, as the first stitch is being moved right along.

Tuck stitch

Tuck stitch is the most common textured stitch used on the machine and it gives a nice crunchy look to the knitting. Set the carriage to tuck and select your punchcard carefully. The holes in the card are the needles which will knit normally. The needles which will tuck are those that are left unmarked. Do not choose a card which has large unpunched areas on it. Most machines will tuck two stitches side by side but they will not do more than this as long tangled loops will result. For the electronic machine it is necessary only to mark the needles required to tuck on the pattern sheet. The pattern can then be reversed so that the unmarked squares will knit. The small tuck stitch pattern for this garment could be elongated to give a more pronounced effect, if using a finer yarn.

Bobbles

These are made by knitting more rows over groups of three needles than on the rest of the row.

It can be done by the following methods:

1 By pulling the needles forward and knitting the extra rows by hand. Different colours could be used for each bobble.

2 By pushing the needles each side to holding position and knitting the bobble with the carriage.

Left like this the extra rows have simply made a little loop of knitting. To stop it from flattening, the bobble needs some stitches behind it.

For a bobble on the knit side of the work

1 The simplest method is to pick up the first row of bobble stitches onto the needles, making a little hem. This closes up the back.

2 The second method makes a more rounded bobble. Take off the two outside stitches from the needles to be used, thread them onto a piece of yarn or a cocktail stick, and allow them to fall

below the knitting, then e-wrap cast-on over the needles (two stitches in centre). Knit the required rows then put both side stitches onto the centre needle(s) and replace the stitches from the cocktail stick onto the empty needles.

For a bobble on the purl side of the work

1 Make a hem with the bobble, but it must protrude in the opposite direction. After knitting the bobble, take the stitches off the needles onto a three-pronged transfer tool, push them well up the prongs and pull the knitting forward. Push the three prongs through the knitting at the base of the bobbles, on the knit side of the work. It is not necessary to try to pick up the exact stitches – in fact it is easier to pick up the bars between the stitches. Place these onto the needles and slide the stitches off on top of them. This has closed the bobble on the knit side.

2 This is the same as the second method for a bobble on the knit side of the work, except that when the side stitches of the bobble are placed on the centre needle, knit all the stitches together with the yarn and take the stitch off the needle. Replace side stitches behind bobble, then replace centre stitch.

Textured jacket pattern

To fit	81	86	91	97	cm
	32	34	36	38	in.

Materials Using three contrasting textured yarns, approx 250gm of main yarn A, 200gm each of yarns B and C. Suggestions for this design: Silverknit Yarns – A Cotton, B Marrakesh and C Pearl, all 4-ply yarns

Tension 27 sts to 10cm (4 in.) measured over st st and approx 75 rows over pattern (rather difficult to measure different stitch patterns). MT approx 6

PATTERN NOTES

1 The punchcard is marked to show where each pattern ends. Mark the beginning of each pattern at the side of the card, at the row *you will see as you knit*. It is important to do this because the carriage setting changes with every pattern, and if you lose

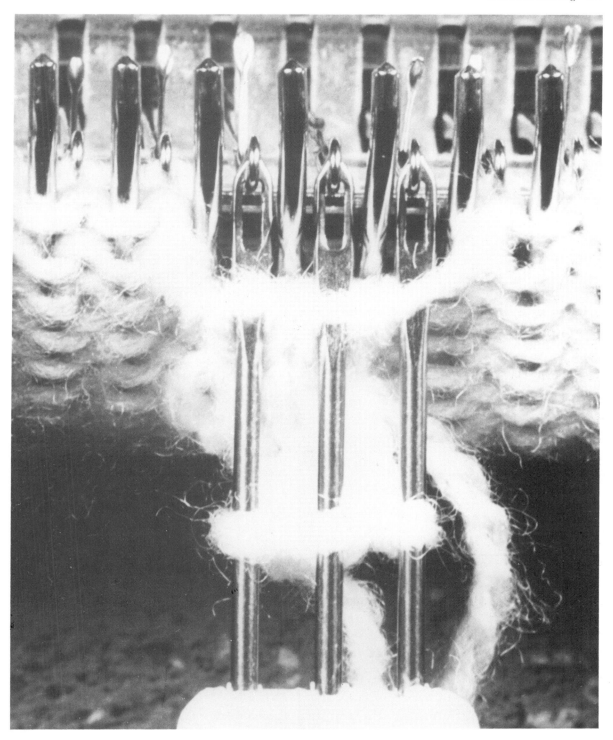

92 Making a bobble which will stand out on the purl side of the fabric. The stitches used to knit the bobble are removed onto the transfer tool which is inserted into the bars between the stitches at the base of the bobble and they are all replaced onto the needles

count of the rows you will still see when you have reached the position to change from slip to tuck, etc. and where to change the yarn.

2 Turn the card round and mark the first rows in the same way, beginning at the opposite ends of the patterns. This will be needed for the second half of each sleeve.

3 The yarn changes all come at the same side of the knitting. Make sure on the fronts that this is the side seam edge. This may mean knitting an extra row on the second front, or beginning at the opposite end, to avoid having a lot of ends where the band fits. It is not possible to e-wrap and fasten all the threads at the end of the rows, because they will show on the right side.

4 When using a silky yarn, pull the knitting down, or weight it lightly. It is very springy and could jump off the needles.

5 Instructions are given for the sleeve width as it was knitted in the example (fig. 93). If you wish to make it wider or narrower you can begin it at any point on the pattern to coincide with the patterns of the back and fronts. The pattern must run straight across the front, back and sleeve.

Keep a check as you knit that the patterns and yarns match up with those on the back and fronts, so that you do not make a mistake in the order. If you made a mistake on the body of the garment, it must be repeated on the sleeves.

6 When shaping sideways-knitted sleeves using holding position, work out the number of rows required at the shoulder and at the cuff. The difference between these is the number of rows to be lost by holding stitches. For example, 100 rows needed at wrist, 150 rows at shoulder. For every 10 rows knitted at shoulder only 5 are needed at wrist. So stitches need to be put into holding position on every alternate row.

7 To sew up, trim all ends to about 8cm (3 in.) and tie any silky yarns together to prevent the end stitches from unravelling. Stitch in the ends close to the edge. An alternative way to deal with them is to sew two rows of a narrow zig-zag stitch on the sewing machine, close to the edge. The ends are then well anchored and can be cut off closely. Make sure that this stitching is hidden within the seam.

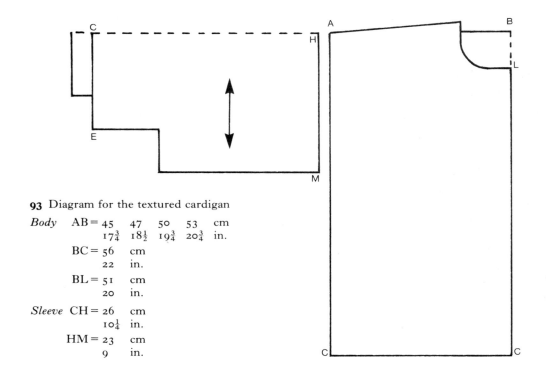

93 Diagram for the textured cardigan

Body	AB =	45	47	50	53	cm
		$17\frac{3}{4}$	$18\frac{1}{2}$	$19\frac{3}{4}$	$20\frac{3}{4}$	in.
	BC =	56				cm
		22				in.
	BL =	51				cm
		20				in.
Sleeve	CH =	26				cm
		$10\frac{1}{4}$				in.
	HM =	23				cm
		9				in.

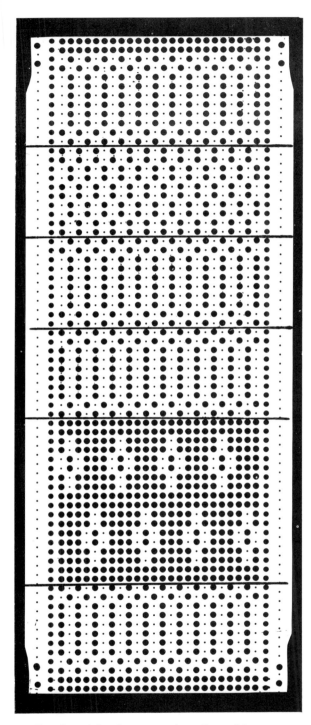

94 Punchcard for the textured cardigan. Lines across the card indicate the start and finish of each pattern section. Mark the card the appropriate number of rows up from the line for your machine to read the first row

BACK
Insert punchcard and lock on row 1.
Using WY cast on 123 129 135 143 sts.
Knit a few rows, change to MY A and MT − 1.
Knit 10 rows. Knit 1 tight row for fold.
RC 000.
Change to MT, knit 4 rows, engage punchcard and knit selecting row. Release card. Set carr to *slip*.
Knit 10 rows.
RC 15.
Change to yarn B. Set carr to *tuck*.
Knit 18 rows.
RC 33.
* Change to yarn C. Set carr to *slip*.
Knit 10 rows.
RC 43.
Lock card and cancel slip setting.
Change to yarn A and knit 7 rows st st, making bobbles on 4th row over sts 9, 10, 11: 15, 16, 17: 22, 23, 24: 35, 36, 37: 41, 42, 43: 47, 48, 49 to right and left of 0.
Engage punchcard and knit 1 row to select needles.
RC 51.
Change to yarn B. Release card and set carr to *slip*.
Knit 10 rows.
RC 61.
Change to yarn C. Set carr to *tuck*.
Knit 10 rows.
RC 71.
Change to yarn A. Set carr to *slip*.
Knit 10 rows.
RC 81.
Lock punchcard. Cancel carr settings.
Change to yarn B and knit 7 rows st st.
RC 88.
Engage card and knit 1 more row to select needles.
Change to yarn C. Set carr to *slip*.
Knit 10 rows.
RC 99.
Change to yarn A. Set carr to *tuck*.
Knit 18 rows. Change to yarn C.
RC 117.**
Continue with sequence of changing yarns and patterns from * to ** until RC 420 is reached.
Take off centre 42 sts onto WY.
Knit on left side only. Continuing in pattern, push 10 needles at shoulder edge to HP for 3 alt rows. Knit 1 row across needles. Cast off round sinker pins. Repeat for other shoulder.

RIGHT FRONT

Cast on with WY 61 65 67 71 sts.
Knit in pattern as for back to RC 365.

Shape neck

Continuing in pattern, push 10 sts at neck edge to HP and wrapping inside needle every time, put 1 needle to HP on next 11 rows (40 44 46 50 sts).
Continue straight in pattern, hanging claw weight next to sts in HP to RC 420.
Shape shoulder as back. Cast off.
Knit right front to match, reversing shaping.

SLEEVES

Shape cuff end of sleeve by putting needles to HP on tuck and st st patterns only (not on the slip hems) in the following sequence:
Push 20 sts to HP at cuff. Knit 2 rows, always wrapping inside needle in HP.
Push next 10 needles to HP. Knit 2 rows.
Push HP needles to UWP, and knit 2 rows across all needles. (If it is a tuck pattern these sts will only knit in st st on first row – on next row they will tuck.) Continue to shape like this until a slip pattern is reached. Do not make bobbles in area of shaping. When shaping cuff at right side, use the following needles:
At left of 0: 7, 8, 9: 19, 20, 21: 36, 37, 38: 42, 43, 44: 48, 49, 50.
At right of 0: 9, 10, 11: 15, 16, 17: 21, 22, 23.
Reverse the left and right for other sleeve, with cuff on right.

Cast on 125 sts with WY.
Change to MY and MT. Engage punchcard on pattern 1.
Beginning with yarn A, knit 1 row in st st. Change to *slip* and knit 10 rows.
Lock card, change to yarn B and knit 7 rows.
Engage punchcard, knit 1 row. Change to yarn C and slip setting, knit 10 rows.
Change to yarn A and tuck.
Continue in pattern in this sequence to RC 195.
Make a row of bobbles in yarn A along this row, which should be the last row of yarn B in st st. This is halfway across the sleeve.
Take out the punchcard and turn it over so that it will revolve in the opposite direction. Lock on first row, which will be the first pattern on the other end of the card.
Knit 7 rows st st in yarn B. Engage punchcard and knit next (selection) row.
Change to yarn A and *slip* setting.
Continue in pattern until RC 195 is reached, finishing with st st in yarn A.
Pick up first row of sleeve onto needles, draw sts through one another and cast off loosely.
Knit second sleeve to match, reversing shapings.

NECKBAND

With wrong (knit) side facing, pick up a total of approx 134 sts around the neck.
Knit a band 12 rows wide, gradually decreasing to MT − 3 and increasing it again over the second half of the band to MT. Pick up sts from first row and cast off round sinker pins or take off on WY and stitch down.

BAND FOR RIGHT FRONT

With wrong (knit) side of work facing, pick up approx 132 sts evenly along front edge. Do not pick up any sts from hem rows at bottom, but do include half of neckband.
RC 000.
Knit 5 rows.
Beginning with 4th needle from edge at the neck end, and at 15-needle intervals, make machine-finished buttonholes over sets of 4 or 5 needles.
RC 10.
Knit 1 tight fold row.
Knit 5 rows. Complete buttonholes.
Knit 5 rows. Finish as on neckband. Repeat band for the left front omitting buttonholes.

CUFFS

Pick up 70 sts from edge of sleeve, gathering in at the ends of the slip-stitch rows.
Knit in st st MT − 2. Knit 40 rows. Knit 1 loose row.
Knit 40 rows. Finish as for bands.

TO MAKE UP

Stitch seams and sew on buttons to correspond with buttonholes.

Decorative hems

Picking up stitches from a few rows below the needles will make a small hem or ridge on the knit side of the fabric. The stitches are easier to pick up in a straight line if a second colour is used to

95 Decorative hems. *Top* Twisted hems made by picking up the stitches several needles to the right or left   *Centre* Short hems made over a few stitches must be balanced to give the same length across the knitting, by repeating across the width   *Bottom* Hems made by picking up a few stitches and leaving a gap mark the row. Striped knitting can be used when several hems are to be made.

For a hem all along the row, every stitch should be picked up. Several hems close together can accentuate an area of the garment, for example at the shoulders.

If several stitches are picked up, then a gap is left of several needles. The knitting will flatten in between the hems to give a varied texture.

Try picking up the stitches diagonally. Instead of placing directly onto the needle above, place each stitch five or six needles to the right. For the next hem place it on needles to the left. This gives the hems a twisted appearance.

Short ridges are made by picking up a few stitches only on the row. The next ridge should be made in another position across the row, so that by the time the garment is finished the same number of rows has been knitted over the full width.

CHAPTER 10

Handspun yarns

Generally, handspun wools are not as even as commercially produced yarns. Often they are thicker and more hairy, and since every spinner's yarn is different, some experimentation will be needed to achieve approximate tension for the pattern given. Any unevenness can be compensated for by plying the wools, the thick part of one thread coinciding with the thinner lengths of the second. A 2-ply yarn will knit more evenly, but is usually too thick to knit on a standard-gauge machine. It can be knitted on alternate needles, although this limits the size that can be made, or it can be used for knitweaving. Singles yarn will knit very well on the machine, but there is one disadvantage: knitted in stocking stitch the resulting fabric will be on the bias. Because the yarn is all twisted in the same direction, and is always thrown off the needles on the machine in the same direction, it will not knit straight. When it is taken off the machine the 'square' knitted will be a diamond shape. The knitting can be blocked out and pressed to shape, using plenty of steam and heat, and this will help to stabilize it. This treatment will pull the pieces into shape, but it is not as permanent as professionally finished fabric, and the garment may need to be pressed into shape each time it is washed. A yarn which is loosely spun will keep its shape better than one with a tight twist.

If the yarn is knitted in a rib this problem does not arise, and one way of getting a stable, even fabric on the single bed machine is to knit a design using two strands together, such as a Fair Isle pattern. The garment pieces will stay in shape very well. If you do not wish to have a multi-coloured garment, then use card 1 (alternate nee-dles selected) and knit using a Fair Isle setting on the carriage with two yarns of the same colour. This is a way of making a thicker fabric from thin yarns. Where there are thinner, weaker lengths of wool, they may break while knitting. Beware of this: knit slowly and watch the wool. Sometimes hairs catch on the needle hooks or sinker pins and jerk the wool, breaking it, or cause uneven stitches. To avoid this and to make the wool run smoothly through the machine, use a silicone spray on each ball. This is very economical to use – only one short burst top and bottom of each ball is needed. Use it also on commercial yarns which are thick or hairy.

Fair Isle waistcoat

| *To fit* | 86–91 | 96–102 | cm |
| | 34–36 | 38– 40 | in. |

Materials Approx 200gm dark wool, 150gm light wool

Tension 28 sts and 34 rows to 10cm (4 in.) at MT approx 9

PATTERN NOTES

1 The original of this pattern was made using a Jacob's sheep fleece which was sorted, the dark wool being spun separately from the cream.

2 The armbands and front bands should be made so that they cover the edges. Because of the uneven nature of most handspun you may find that the edges are wavy. The double band will cover this up.

3 The punchcard uses traditional Fair Isle patterns.

4 If you use this pattern to knit with commercial rather than handspun yarns, you may find that you need to knit more rows to give the correct length.

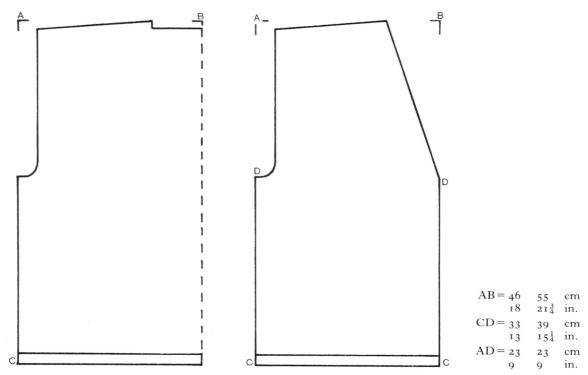

AB = 46 55 cm
     18 21¾ in.
CD = 33 39 cm
     13 15¼ in.
AD = 23 23 cm
      9   9 in.

96 Diagram for the Fair Isle waistcoat, knitted using singles handspun wool

BACK
Using WY cast on 129 154 sts. Knit a few rows.
Change to MY dark and MT − 2.
Knit 22 rows. Knit 1 loose fold row. Knit 22 rows MT − 1.
RC 000.
Change to MT. Knit 3 rows.
Lock on card and knit 1 row.
Release card. Set carr for Fair Isle.
Continue to knit in pattern to RC 114 134.

Shape armholes
Cast off 6 8 sts at beg of next 2 rows.
Continue to knit in pattern to RC 195 209.

Shape shoulders and back neck
Cast off 50 sts in centre. Continue on left side.
Knit 6 rows, pushing 6 needles to HP at shoulder on every alt row.

Knit 1 row across all needles. Take off on WY, or cast off.
Complete right side to match.

FRONTS
Cast on with WY 65 80 sts.
Make a hem as for back and continue in pattern to RC 114 134.

Shape front and armholes
Dec 1 st at beg of next row. Knit 1 row.
Cast off 6 8 sts at beg of next row.
Cont in pattern, dec 1 st at centre front at beg of every 5th row to 45 sts.
Knit to RC 195 209 and shape shoulder as for back.
Knit right front to match, reversing shapings.
Graft or stitch shoulder seams.

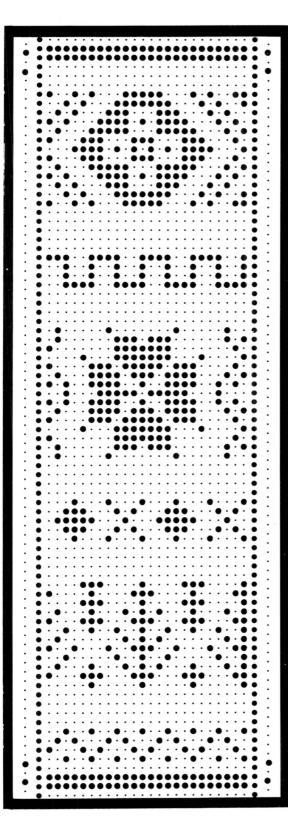

97 A selection of traditional Fair Isle patterns as used for the handspun waistcoat

ARMHOLES

Pick up approx 124 140 sts round the armhole.
Knit 10 rows, gradually dec from MT to MT − 2.
Knit 1 loose row. Knit 10 rows, gradually inc to MT.

FRONT BANDS

Knit in 2 halves.
Pick up approx 166 188 sts along front edge and halfway across back neck.
Knit 12 rows at MT−1. Knit 1 loose row. Knit 12 rows at MT−2.
Take off on WY and stitch down inside.

Woven coat

The second and perhaps the easiest way to use handspun yarns on the machine is for weaving. The wools originally used for this coat were plied and chunky, and the knitting yarn was a 4-ply thickness wool, so it makes a very warm, thick garment.

The weaving wools were also sprayed with silicone spray as they were rather hairy, and although they were not looping through the needles, the fibres did catch on the sinker pins.

Because the handspun is very thick the pattern is designed to be knitted only on alternate needles. Do not count the needles in non-working position. This pattern could be used to knit some of the commercially spun bouclé chunky yarns, the alternate needles giving space for the extra-thick yarn.

To fit   96–101   cm
            36– 40   in.

Materials Approx 600gm 2-ply handspun in three colours: A alpaca, B camel hair, C mohair; 400gm 2/16 wool, used double (4-ply)

Tension   14 sts and 32 rows to 10cm (4 in.) at MT approx 10

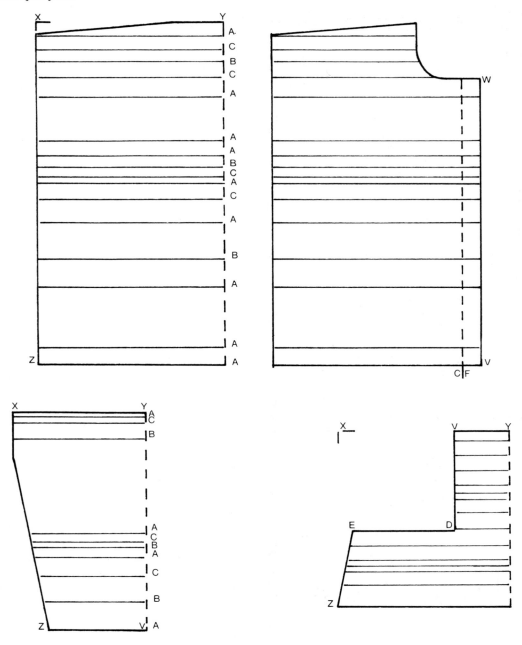

98 Coat woven from handspun wools, using alternate needles. Letters A, B and C indicate the changes of colour

	Body		Sleeve		Hood	
	XY = 30 cm		XY = 22.5 cm		XY = 35.5 cm	
	11¾ in.		8¾ in.		14 in.	
	XZ = 32 cm		XZ = 46 cm		VD = 25 cm	
	12½ in.		18 in.		9¾ in.	
	ZW = 59 cm		ZV = 17 cm		EZ = 20 cm	
	23¼ in.		6¾ in.		8 in.	

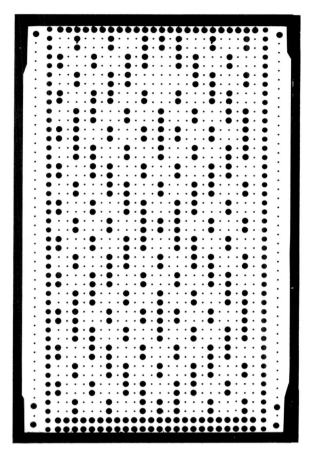

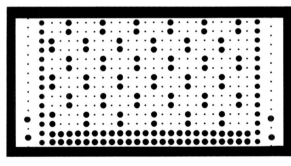

99 Punchcards used for the woven coat

1 used over most of the design
2 the diamond shape, which could be used all over if required

STRIPED PATTERN

Punchcard 1 used unless otherwise indicated.

Back and front from bottom			Sleeve from bottom	
26 rows	A		16 rows	A
46	A	Punchcard 2	16	B
24	A		10	C
24	B		8	A
10	A		4	B
10	C		8	C
2	A		70	A
4	C		8	B
4	B		8	C
10	A			
24	A	Punchcard 2	Hood from face edge	
10	A		18 rows	A
8	C		10	B
8	B		4	A
8	A		12	C
			16	A
			4	B
			Repeat throughout hood	

BACK

Using WY cast on 86 sts over alt needles. Knit a few rows.

Change to knitting yarn and MT − 2.

Knit 10 rows. Engage punchcard, lock on row 1.
RC 000.

At MT knit 1 row.

Release card and weave in pattern as chart to RC 210.

Shape shoulders by pushing 8 needles to HP opposite carr on next 8 rows.

Mark 14 sts each side of 0 for neck and cast off.

FRONTS

Using WY cast on 56 sts over alt needles. Knit a few rows.

Change to knitting yarn and continue as back to RC 146.

Cast off 16 sts.

Dec 1 st at beg of alt rows to 29 sts.

Knit to RC 210.

Shape shoulders as back and cast off.

Repeat for second front, reversing shapings.

SLEEVE

Using WY cast on 48 sts over alt needles. Knit a few rows.

Change to knitting yarn and MT − 1.

Knit 10 rows.

Engage punchcard, lock on row 1.

At MT knit 1 row.

Inc 1 st at beg of 7th and 8th rows to 64 sts.

Knit to RC 148.

Cast off.

HOOD

Using WY cast on 100 sts over alt needles. Knit a few rows.

Change to knitting yarn and MT.

Engage card, lock on row 1.

Knit 1 row. Release card and begin weaving.

Dec 1 st at beg of every 9th and 10th row to 90 sts.

Continue in weaving pattern to RC 64.

Cast off 34 sts at beg of next row.

Knit 1 row. Cast off 34 sts at beg of next row.

Knit 80 rows on remaining 22 sts in centre.

Cast off.

TO MAKE UP

Turn in the front of the hood for 3cm (1¼ in.) and stitch down. Stitch the shoulders.

Join the seams up the back of hood and sew onto the neckline, leaving 6cm (2½ in.) at each front edge for the overlap fastening.

Sew the sleeve and side seam. Turn front edge under for 3cm (1¼ in.) and stitch down. Sew on frog fastenings.

Patch pockets can be added:

Cast on 21 sts over alt needles and weave at MT for 56 rows. Turn over 2cm (¾ in.) at top for welt, and sew onto the fronts.

The pockets will not stretch out of shape if a lining fabric is sewn inside.

It is possible to produce deliberately textured yarns when spinning your own by wrapping one thread round another, or allowing one of the yarns to overtwist and loop. Slub yarns look very effective – not always made deliberately, especially by beginners! These yarns are thicker than the singles used for the Fair Isle pattern, partly because of their design and partly because they are usually plied. They can often be knitted on every needle at the largest tension if they are not too hairy. They can certainly be knitted on alternate needles, like the woven coat, for which the wool is very thick. If they come somewhere in between then try knitting on two out of three needles in stocking stitch. This gives some spare yarn in the ladders between the stitches, and a good downwards tug after knitting will make the stitches take up some of this slack so that the knitting does not feel too stiff.

Use the basic block for a pattern. If there are not enough needles to knit the whole of one section (a back or a front) in one piece on alternate needles, then rearrange the pattern to accommodate this. Half the front could be knitted from bottom to top, and the other half knitted sideways, or the whole garment could be knitted sideways. Try knitting the front in four squares, each one a different stitch pattern. There is always a way to get round it and handspun yarn *will* knit most successfully on the machine.

CHAPTER 11

Experiments and decorations

There are two ways to change the colours of the yarns you use. One is by dyeing them before knitting, and the other is to colour the knitted fabric afterwards.

Dyeing

If you spin your own wool you will no doubt have experimented with dyes, but many knitters never try it. The effects can be stunning and a garment knitted from hand-dyed yarn will be unique.

Many dyes are poisonous, so sensible precautions should be taken. Since it will probably be carried out in your kitchen, ensure that foodstuffs and eating utensils are well out of the way. Wear rubber gloves and an apron, or old clothes – or both. Some dyes come as powders. Try not to sprinkle them too wildly and if using them in any quantity a mask should be worn. Certainly take care not to inhale them.

Synthetic yarns need dyes specially formulated for them. They may colour a little, from the dyes described here, but not so easily as natural fibres. It is advisable to use wool or cotton which colour easily with most types of dye. Part of the fun of dyeing your own yarns is that you can never be *absolutely* certain of the result. The hardness, or softness, of the water will affect the colour and the slightest variation in dye quantities will make a huge difference. Ideally you should use a stainless steel or unchipped enamel pan. In fact most people use any old pan they have, so the aluminium or iron of the vessel will also affect the colour acquired. Don't be put off – a blue dye will still give a kind of blue and a red one will still be red.

Begin by winding the small amounts left over from the knitting projects into skeins and experiment with these. Tie the skeins loosely but securely with a figure-of-eight tie in several places. If you don't do this the wool will tangle and hours of your time will be wasted trying to rewind it. The figure-of-eight tie will not slide up the skein. Try winding two or three yarns together. If they are different fibres, for example wool, cotton, acrylic, then they will each take up the dye to a different degree and an interesting shaded yarn could result.

If you are using up your oddments then the original colour of the yarn will make a difference to the final colour after dyeing. This will be very much a matter of trial and error. A yellow yarn dyed with blue will end up green. A pink yarn could be dyed a deeper shade of red, but adding blue to the dye bath may result in a lavender yarn.

You may think it a lot of trouble to have to wind the wool twice, once into a skein and again into a ball for knitting, so try dyeing balls as they are. The dye will not penetrate so easily and a yarn in various shades will result. If your wool is wound onto plastic cones then the whole cone can be dipped into the dye with the same shaded result, though only use small cones to do this. It takes longer for balls and cones to dry. Place them in an old pillowcase and spin-dry them well. Hang them outside, inside a vegetable net to dry.

Shetland wool in skeins can be purchased from Jamieson and Smith in natural colours. This is very good to use for more accurate dyeing. However, even using a white wool and measuring everything carefully, it is almost impossible to repeat a colour exactly. So if you want to make a complete garment in your dyed wool, *all* of it must be dyed in the same bath at the same time. This demands a large vessel, but a few individually-dyed ounces of wool can be used for trimmings, Fair Isle patterns, two-colour tuck, etc.

100 Figure-of-eight tie to hold yarn securely in a skein

Tie and dye

By binding the skein tightly in two or three places the dye is prevented from penetrating and patches of the original colour will be left. Knotting the skein will also result in different shades of colour where the dye only partially penetrates the knot.

Space dyeing

If the skein is suspended over the dye bath so that only half of it is immersed in the liquid, the top part will not be coloured, the middle will be pale where the dye has seeped up the fibres and the bottom will be a deeper colour. The wool can be left like this, or the skein can be reversed in another colour so that the top remains colour A,

the centre is a paler mixture of A and B, and the bottom is dyed with colour B.

Natural dyes

There are many very good and more specialized books on vegetable dyeing so details are not given here, but a few notes are included to encourage you to try it.

All plant material will provide a dye of some sort. The colours are usually rather gentle, subtle shades which blend well together. All parts of a plant can be used: leaves, flowers, berries, roots, stems. The colours are unpredictable and sometimes rather surprising. Beetroot, for example, does not always give a red, but more often an orange/yellow.

Plant dyes with a few exceptions are not fast, so the wool must be mordanted. A mordant is a substance which combines with the fibres and the dye substance to make the colour permanent. Salt can be used, or vinegar. Alum (potassium aluminium sulphate) can be obtained from the chemist and this is commonly used. To mordant 250gm wool about 80gm alum is needed. Add a teaspoon of cream of tartar to the bath to keep the wool soft and dissolve these in 4 litres of water.

The wool must be wet before it is placed in the bath, which must be big enough for the yarn to float and for the liquid to circulate freely. If it is not, then patchy colours will result. The wool is simmered in the mixture for about an hour. Do not stir or agitate too much, but just give an occasional swish. The wool can then be dried and kept until it is convenient to dye it, or placed straight into the dye bath.

The plant material should be boiled and well crushed to get as much colour from the plant fibres as possible. The actual material can be removed from the bath before the wool is added, or it can be left in. If it is a type of substance which will tangle in the wool then it can be put into a muslin bag. The dye is usually stronger if the plant is left in the bath.

The mordant used will alter the final colour produced – yet another factor to consider. The sleeveless pullover in plate 13 has a Fair Isle design on it taken from the Regine Faust pattern punchcard designs (from Metropolitan Sewing Machines). It is knitted in wool that is all dyed with elderberries, using three different mordants.

The palest has had vinegar added to the dye bath, the brown/pink used alum, and the deepest purple used oxalic acid. This has produced three colours, all different yet all blending well together. The garment was knitted on a standard-gauge machine.

Vegetable dyeing is cheap. Oxalic acid mordant is obtained from rhubarb leaves. If you pickle onions you will have plenty of skins and with alum these give fast colours of lovely yellows and oranges. Privet hedge clippings make a paler yellow, blackberries a blue-grey. Do experiment – if you don't like the result, re-dye in another colour, or by another method.

Rainbow dyes

(see Suppliers on p. 139

With these chemical dyes it is simple and straight-forward to dye natural fibres. Paler colours can also be obtained on some synthetics. Fleeces can be dyed unwashed before spinning and it is a trouble-free method. The results with these dyes are dramatic, and the colours clear and fast. They can be used on hand-spun and on commercially spun yarns.

Several different colours can be used in one dye bath. Where they merge yet more colours are produced. It is the unusual method of dyeing which creates the interesting effects. The dyes are strong and should be used sparingly. They are therefore very economical.

During the dyeing process the dyestuffs are sprinkled directly onto the moistened yarns, which are crammed *tightly* into the pan. In this case no room is left for the yarns and liquid to circulate. As the pan is gently heated the dyestuffs literally run into one another. Strong or subtle shadings and striking blends of colours are thus produced. Gentle but thorough rinsing ensures good colourfastness.

Commercially spun yarns which have some wool in them, even a small percentage, will take up the dye very well. Hand-knitting yarns may be left in the loosely wound balls.

The colours are not repeatable. In fact they vary from ball to ball and from skein to skein in one dye bath. It would be impossible to sprinkle the dye powders in exactly the same quantities over each one. It is the unexpected random results that are so exciting.

Stock solutions can be made, however, which do produce a standard result. Full instructions for several methods of using them are included with the dyes.

Colour plate 10 shows examples of rainbow-dyed skeins.

To knit with dyed wool

Since you will have several balls of yarn which vary in shade and colour from one another, it is necessary to consider the final effect you want. Using one ball after another will result in sudden changes of colour across the garment. Try to blend the colours so that the different balls will merge into one another to give a more gradual change.

To have a general mixture of colour, for example with the Rainbow-dyed yarns, knit two rows with each of up to four balls of yarn. There is no sudden change of colour and the overall effect is of one range of shades. Using a colour changer for this will speed up the knitting.

When using the Rainbow-dyed yarn for Fair Isle – and it is ideal for this, giving multicoloured patterns – use a completely contrasting colour for the background. Using a colour close to any of the shades of the dyed yarn will result in some of the pattern disappearing into the background.

Painting on the knitted surface

Fabric crayons

These can be used to colour small areas of fabrics of all kinds, including knitting. Because it is so stretchy the knitted fabric is quite difficult to colour evenly. Keep all the strokes going the same way and continue in one place until the depth of colour you want is reached. By tacking a piece of cloth behind a small area of knitting it is possible to hold the fabric more firmly, which makes the crayons easier to apply.

The colours can be removed by washing if you make a mistake or change your mind, but when you have decided that the design is correct they are made permanent by ironing with as hot an iron as the fabric will stand over a dry cloth.

Fabric paints

These are applied with a brush, and penetrate the

fibres of the yarn rather better than the crayons. To get even coverage apply the paints a little at a time layer by layer. To avoid getting paint on the other side of the garment, insert a piece of stiff cardboard inside the jumper to stop the paint from seeping through. Leave it inside while the paints are fixed by ironing.

Acrylics do not give a good result with either crayons or paints because not enough heat can be applied to make the colours fast. Cottons, wool and wool mixtures take the colours well. Paints and crayons are available from artists suppliers.

Not all knitting has to be a garment

Here are ideas for two wall hangings.

Flowers

The flowers for the first hanging have all been knitted separately and sewn to the background. The background piece was knitted first. Its finished size is 30cm × 70cm (12 in. × 27½ in.). Add enough stitches to give a turned-back hem at each side of about 3–5cm (1¼–2 in.). Leave a stitch out of work up the edge where the fold is to be made. A hem is made at the top to thread a dowel through for hanging. To make a firmer backing, attach a piece of iron-on interfacing to the back and stitch the side hems down onto this at the back.

TO MAKE THE FLOWERS
Use a fine yarn or the flowers will look clumsy, for example a single strand of 2/30. Cast on about 40 stitches using the weaving cast-on which gives a length of yarn threaded through the first row of stitches. Use a fine tension (about 1 or 2) and knit 20 rows. Push every tenth needle to holding position and set carriage to hold. Knit 2 rows. Change colour to make the coloured tips of the 'petals' and knit 2 rows. Change back to main colour and knit 2 rows. Set carriage to knit back the stitches in holding position and knit 20 rows. Do not cast off but break the yarn leaving about 30cm (12 in.). Thread this through the stitches on the machine. Take the stitches off. Fold the strip of knitting in half and press. Draw up the threads at both edges tightly into the middle. Tie them together, and stitch into place. The side seam can then be sewn up with mattress stitch. Leave one

end of the yarn in the centre for sewing the flower onto the background.

The bells are made in a similar way. Fewer stitches are cast on, but more rows are knitted. Cast on about 18 stitches and knit 30 rows. Knit the edge as before, putting every sixth needle into holding position for 6 rows. Knit 30 rows. Finish as before.

The stalk is sewn-on cord. Small leaves are strips of knitting with a thread tacked along the centre and drawn up slightly to give the crinkled effect. Allow the knitting to roll at the sides. Larger leaves are made from a fine yarn, the points shaped by putting needles to holding position on every row and returning them in the same order. Mattress-stitch the edges.

The flowers could also be sewn onto a garment for decoration, and bells make attractive ends to drawstring cords.

Trees in winter

For this hanging the background piece is knitted as before. A variety of colours is used to give the impression of a sunset landscape. Using different yarns like this means that sometimes the edges are not level – they waver in and out with the different thicknesses of yarns. Turn in the edges in a straight line, and make a hem, for a dowel, top and bottom.

The trees are knitted separately in stocking stitch and sewn on. The knitting is allowed to roll to give the three-dimensional effect of the tree trunks. The trees are knitted in a 4-ply acrylic, about tension 7.

LARGE TREE
Cast on about 24 stitches and knit for 50 rows. Pushing 16 of the needles to holding position, cast on 4 stitches and knit 20 rows on 12 stitches. Divide the work in half again and knit a few rows, divide again and knit about 12 rows on the 3 stitches. Take these off the machine and thread the yarn through them. Return to the other set of stitches, knit about 15 rows on these and take off in the same way. Knit a few rows on next set of 6 stitches. Divide the work again and knit a length on each set of three stitches.

Return to the original 16 stitches and knit 20 rows. Divide the work again irregularly to knit more branches. You are creating the tree as you

101 Flower wall hanging. The flowers are made separately and the caterpillar at the top is a cord

102 Trees in winter. The background is knitted in stripes to give the appearance of a sunset and the trees are knitted separately

knit in a random manner. If, when you come to sew it on, it does not have enough branches, knit a few more rows over 3 or 4 stitches and attach to the tree.

Smaller trees are made by casting on fewer stitches and knitting fewer rows.

Try a dark background and pale-coloured trees.

The trees seem rather muddled when they are knitted and there are lots of ends hanging from them, but these can be used to sew the trees to the background.

Appliqué

The introduction of Bondaweb has made this an easy way of decorating knitwear or making pictures. A strip of knitting can be made and the Bondaweb ironed onto the reverse side. Keep the paper backing in place and draw onto it the shape you want. Use a template if you want several identical pieces – perhaps for flower petals. The knitting and backing can be cut out to the shape you want without any danger of it fraying. The paper is pulled off and the pieces can then be sewn to a garment using a satin stitch on the sewing machine. Alternatively, the shape can be sewn round on the sewing machine. The Bondaweb prevents it from stretching out of shape, and the surplus is cut off afterwards. The motif can be attached in one or two places – it need not be sewn flat onto the surface of the knitting – giving a more three-dimensional appearance. Try making the trees for the wall hanging like this if you don't want to knit every branch separately.

Embroidery on knitting

Satin stitch, french knots and bullion stitch are the stitches most commonly used to decorate knitwear. They look very effective. An embroidered collar or pocket can lift a garment out of the ordinary. Wool to match the garment can be used, or cottons or silks to give a contrast. A Fair Isle design of flowers can be enhanced by adding embroidery to the centres of some of the flowers.

Swiss darning has been used on the Continent to decorate knitting for many years. As well as adding complete motifs to a garment it is useful for rectifying any mistakes in a Fair Isle pattern, perhaps where a dropped stitch has not been picked up correctly. Bring the needle up in the centre of the stitch and take it down through the centre of the stitch to the right and two rows up. Bring the needle up in the next stitch on the left and back down into the first one. The embroidery thread has imitated the shape of the knitting stitch in the same way as when grafting two pieces of knitting together.

Decorating with beads

Very small beads have to be sewn onto the knitted fabric afterwards, but those with a large enough hole in the middle can be attached directly while knitting.

Thread the bead onto a fine crochet hook (1.5 mm or less). Lift the stitch off the needle with the hook and slide the bead down over the complete stitch. Replace the stitch onto the needle above the bead and knit the next row. This technique can be used for attaching lengths of lace and other articles with a large enough hole, e.g. small rings or bells.

If using the purl side of the fabric as the right side, beads can be threaded onto a length of yarn and woven into the knitting. Thread several pieces of yarn, or narrow ribbon, with the beads and either by hand, or using a punchcard, select alternate needles. With the weaving brushes in position, lay the yarn across the needles. The yarn can go right across the row and be sewn in at the sides, or use shorter lengths and allow the ends to hang loosely, as shown in fig. 103.

Another way of decorating the purl side of the knitting, perhaps between areas of tuck, slip or weaving, is by using wrapping patterns. Select the needles to be used and move to D or E position. These can be in groups or several needles apart, or using alternate needles. With a contrast yarn, e-wrap the selected needles on top of the stitches. Do not pull the winding yarn too tight or it will be difficult to knit the row. A variety of patterns can be made like this – the yarn can be wrapped round some needles twice, or round two together. Two will give a more knobbly effect. Loops will trail between needles which have longer gaps between them and wrapping alternate rows in different directions will give yet another pattern.

To add these weaving and winding patterns to a stocking stitch jumper which you wish to wear with the knit side outside, turn the work over using yarn or the garter bar. Knit the rows with the pattern, then reverse again so that you continue with purl side facing.

By using your own choice of yarn, colour and stitch pattern your knitwear is already very individual and interpreting some of the ideas in your own way will certainly make it your own design.

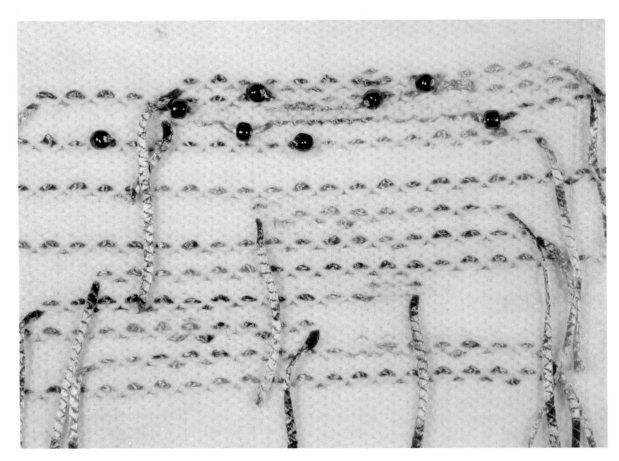

103 Weaving in a decorative ribbon-like yarn for a few stitches with ends left to hang. Atkinsons Reflections was used for this piece. At the top, beads are threaded onto it and knitted in at intervals

104 Wrapping patterns on the surface of the purl side of the knitting. The yarn can be wrapped round two needles together, or allowed to loop from alternate needles, or a simple e-wrap can be used, in either direction

FURTHER READING

BROTHER, *Knitting Techniques Book*, Brother Industries Ltd, Japan, 1984.

COMPTON, Rae, *The Complete Book of Traditional Knitting*, Batsford, 1983.

DAVIS, Johanna, *Machine Knitting to Suit Your Mood*, Pelham, 1982.

KINDER, Kathleen, *A Resource Book for Machine Knitters*, 1979. *A Second Resource Book*, 1980. *A Resource Book Pattern Supplement*, 1983. (Available from Kathleen Kinder, Vallew View, Station Road, Giggleswick, Settle, N. Yorkshire, BD24 0AB)

LEWIS, Susannah and WEISSMAN, Julia, *A Machine Knitter's Guide to Creating Fabrics*, Lark Books, USA, 1986. (Available from the Knitting Neuk, 32 Ashley Road, Aberdeen AB1 6RJ)

McGREGOR, Sheila, *The Complete Book of Traditional Fair Isle Knitting*, Batsford, 1981.

MURRAY, Felicity, *Design Your Own Machine Knitwear*, Foulsham, 1985.

NELSON, Joanna, *More Mysteries of Machine Knitting Unravelled*, 1984. (Available from J. Nelson, 9 Postwood Green, Hertford Heath, Hertford SG13 7QJ.)

WEAVER, Mary, *Machine Knitting Technology and Patterns*, 1979. (Available from Weaverknits, 276–278 Main Road, Sutton-at-Home, Dartford, Kent)

Spinning

CHADWICK, Eileen, *The Craft of Hand Spinning*, Batsford, 1980.

ROSS, Mabel, *The Essentials of Yarn Design for Spinners*, 1983. (Available from Mabel Ross, Crook of Devon, Kinross, Scotland)

Dyeing

GOODWIN, Jill, *The Dyers' Manual*, Pelham, 1982.

THURSTAN, Violetta, *The Use of Vegetable Dyes*, Reeves-Dryad Press, 1977.

Magazines

By subscription

Knitting Machine Digest
144 Frant Road, Thornton Heath, Surrey CR4 7JU

Machine Knitting World
1–2 East Market Street, Newport, Gwent NP9 2AY

Available from newsagents
Machine Knitting News
Machine Knitting Monthly
World of Knitting

Magazines (USA)

Knitting Machine News and Views,
Alles Hutchinson, 315 Hamil Road, Verona, Pa 15147

Machine Knitter's Newsletter, 347 West 39th Street no. 402, New York, NY 10018

Suppliers

UK
Rainbow dyes

Something Sheepy
Ivy House
Dennington Road
Framlingham
Woodbridge
Suffolk IP13 9JL

Yarns and accessories

All the suppliers on this list will send their goods by mail order, and most welcome personal shoppers. Always enclose a stamped addressed envelope when you send for details. Some stockists make a small charge for their samples – this is usually refunded with the first order.

Having a selection of swatches to browse through often provides the inspiration for knitting something new. They show what a great variety of exciting yarns there are now available for us to use. Your local shop cannot stock them all, and many parts of the country have a very limited access to coned yarn.

Atkinsons Yarns
Terry Mills
Horbury
Ossett
W. Yorkshire WF5 9SA
A lovely selection of colours in all yarns. Some also sold in balls if only a small quantity required. Range from 2/30 to chunky

Bedford Sewing and Knitting Ltd (SK)
58 Bronham Road
Bedford MK40 2QB
Stockists of knitting machines, accessories and spare parts. Large selection of quality yarns under own brand name

Jamieson and Smith Ltd
90 North Road
Lerwick
Shetland 2EI OFQ
Genuine Shetland wool in 2-ply (2/8), 450gm on
cone (this knits as a 4-ply wool). Also a lighter lace-weight Shetland wool on skeins of 28gm. All available in natural fleece colours and many lovely shades

Many a Mickle
1 Cobden Street
Darwen
Lancashire BB3 2NY
This is the place to buy pure undyed wools on cones if you don't spin your own. Herdwick, Jacob and Swaledale wools, as well as Shetland and lambswool

Metropolitan Sewing Machines
321 Ashley Road
Parkstone
Poole
Dorset BH14 OAP
Stockist of knitting machines, accessories and spare parts of all machines; Regine Faust and other punchcard designs; and a good selection of books. Large selection of branded yarns – Bramwell, King Cole, Argyll, etc. – as well as their own. Some haberdashery, including fusible nylon. Organizers of the To and Fro Postal Knitters Club

Nantiago Homecrafts
49–50 Frogmore Street
Abergavenny
Gwent NP7 5AN
An excellent, quick service for very large selection of coned yarns from many manufacturers, including Patsy, Forsell and Knitmaster Kone. All at competitive prices. Good descriptive list, but actual samples only available by special request

Silverknit Yarns
Park Road
Calverton
Nottingham NG14 6LL
Yarns on small cones of 200gm in an interesting variety. Cottons, viscose, acrylics and mohairs, mixtures. Reels of toning cotton for punch lace, and a range of lurex glitter yarns. Small charge for samples. (Calverton is where the Revd William Lee lived and invented the knitting machine in 1589.)

Simply Shetland
1 Dalry Road
Haymarket
Edinburgh
Large range of colours of Shetland wool, from several manufacturers, 2/8 Shetland in oil on cones of approx 1kg. Also 3/13 lambswool which knits to same tension. Quantity discount

Texere Yarns
College Mill
Barkerend Road
Bradford BD3 9AQ
Vast range of yarns for knitting and weaving, all on cones. Charge made for samples as there are so many. Worth a personal visit if possible

Uppingham Yarns Market
22 North Street East
Uppingham
Leics LE15 9QL
Very large collection of industrial yarns of all kinds at wholesale prices. Mohairs, cottons, textured wool, 2/30 acrylics in wide range of colours. Trade discount for cottage industries

Machine manufacturers

Jones and Brother
Jones Sewing Machine Co. Ltd
Shepley Street
Guide Bridge
Audenshaw
Manchester M34 5JD

Knitmaster Ltd
39–45 Cowleaze Road
Kingston-upon-Thames
Surrey KT2 6DT

Passap
Bogod Machine Co. Ltd
50–52 Great Sutton Street
London EC1 0DJ

Pfaff Ltd
Pfaff House
East Street
Leeds LS9 8EH

Singer Distribution Ltd
Grafton Way

West Ham Industrial Estate
Basingstoke RG22 6HE

Toyota Sewing and Knitting Machines
34 High Street
Bromley
Kent BR1 1EA

USA
Dyes

Dyekit
412 East 4th Street
Bloomington
IN 47410

Yarns and accessories

Bare Hill Studios (Fiber Loft)
Rt 111 Harvard
MA 01451

Heirloom Yarns
PO Box 239
Rochell IL 61068–0239

Scott's Woollen Mill
Hecla Street and Elmdale Road
Uxbridge MA 01569

Machine manufacturers

Brother machines, Brother International Corp.
8 Corporate Place
Piscataway
NJ 08854

Passap and Superba Machines
Associated Knitting Machine Co. Inc.
1275 Bloomfield Avenue
Building 214
Fairfield
NJ 07006

Singer Company
Dept VK 8/85
135 Raritan Center Parkway
Edison
NJ 08837

Studio Machines
Studio Yarn Farms Inc
10024 14th Avenue SW
Seattle
WA 98146

Toyota Machines
Newton Knits Inc.
3969 East La Palma
Anaheim
CA 92807

INDEX